Big Mac

The Unauthorized Story of McDonald's
by
Max Boas and Steve Chain

E. P. DUTTON AND CO., INC. | NEW YORK | 1976

Chapter 12, "The Politics of Hamburger,"
was previously published in *Swank* magazine
in considerably different form.

LIBRARY OF CONGRESS CATALOGING IN PUBLICATION DATA

Boas, Max.
Big Mac: the unauthorized story of McDonald's.

1. McDonald's System, inc. I. Chain, Steve,
joint author. II. Title.
HD9009.M3B6   1975   338.7′66′47940975   75–15988

10 9 8 7 6 5 4 3 2

Published simultaneously in Canada by Clarke, Irwin & Company
Limited, Toronto and Vancouver
ISBN: 0-525-06675-6

Contents

Big Mac

Danny Dreamer

"This Is Rat Eat Rat, Dog Eat Dog"

Ray Albert Kroc was born on October 5, 1902, in Oak Park, a respectable lower-middle-class neighborhood on Chicago's West Side. The neighborhood consisted mostly of Germans and Slavs. The Bohemian immigrants among them were known as "Bohunks," many of them laborers in stockyards and factories. A number of these Bohemians rose from their immigrant ghettos and made their mark on the city. George Halas became known as the hard-charging owner of the Chicago Bears; another Bohemian, Anton Cermak, became mayor of Chicago in 1931 as the result of a political alliance that established the so-called ethnically balanced ticket, a strategy that would be followed faithfully by Chicago's successive city machines. Ray Kroc was also a Bohemian, a Bohunk, as he proudly calls himself.

Kroc's grandfather had been killed in one of the many obscure European upheavals that shook the crumbling Austro-

Hungarian Empire toward the end of the nineteenth century. Fleeing her native Bohemia (now part of Czechoslovakia), his grandmother arrived in the United States in the early 1890s. For a while she and her four children lived in a basement flat at Chicago Avenue and Wells Street. Everybody in the family pitched in to survive. Ray Kroc's father had to go to work at the age of twelve, first for Western Union and then for a subsidiary, ADT, American District Telegraph.

From his early days Ray Kroc witnessed the fierce contest for the rare prizes of the marketplace and the even more ruthless struggle not to sink any lower into poverty. His father, with only the benefit of a grammar-school education, worked himself up to secretary-treasurer with the telegraph company. Forever trying to better himself, he began buying up real estate in 1925; at the same time he warned his son, "Don't buy any oil wells. Don't get mixed up with these stockbrokers. You go, you walk on the ground. You look at it. It's solid. Real estate is the basis."

But the real estate business went downhill, and as the family struggled to maintain its newly won respectability, the depression engulfed them. In 1932 Kroc's father died of a cerebral hemorrhage at the desk of the Pyramid Vacant Real Estate Company, leaving little money. Ironically, as the bad times got worse, vacant real estate began to boom shortly afterward. "Timing is such a factor in life," Ray Kroc later said.

At age four his father took him to a phrenologist. Hands were laid on the small round skull and it was pronounced that he would make his fortune in either music or food. And music did become Ray Kroc's first love. His mother showed him the scales, and on cold winter days when the wind blew off the lake, he sat in the half-light in an overstuffed room, earnestly hammering at the classics.

But soon he found his second great passion. He opened a popcorn stand, and a lemonade stand, while his grandfather would occasionally peer over his newspaper at the busy little vendor and jokingly call him "Danny Dreamer"—after a popular comic strip character of the time. Danny Dreamer's other love was selling.

An indifferent student, Ray Kroc was impatient in school. He had come into the world under the aegis of a spreading imperial power, ruled by the Bull Moose President. A Hudson Valley patrician with perfect white teeth and poor eyes who believed in the "strenuous life," Rough Riders, "strong men," and "the doer of the deeds," Theodore Roosevelt ballyhooed the singular titan, the rugged individualist who was held up as the cream of the species: ". . . the man who is actually in the arena, whose face is marred by dust and sweat and blood. . . ."

Ray Kroc had the full quotation framed and hung in his office more than a half century later, the same words quoted by Richard Nixon in a tearful speech to his White House staff on the morning of his resignation as President of the United States.

They were words that thrilled Ray as a boy, just as he was moved when he heard President Wilson sound a romantic and stirring note to fight a war that would end all wars. To Ray Kroc, World War I was also a chance to learn to drive the automobile. When he was still a month shy of enlistment age, his parents allowed him to quit school and join the Red Cross. He had just turned sixteen when a gray troopship took him to France. He was a small, skinny, quick-witted youngster. Like most of the enlistees, he did not know what the fighting was all about, but in France he learned to drive an automobile with a cargo of wounded and dying, an ambulance with black flags plowing between mud-filled trenches.

Ray Kroc's outfit was Company A, the first to be organized, and in it he met an enlistee by the name of Walt Disney, a fellow-Chicagoan who also drove an ambulance. The two never got to be close. Walt spent his off-duty hours in the barracks, doodling a bizarre bestiary of little monsters, and

Ray Kroc left the ambulance corps soon after volunteering for special duty. This consisted of playing the piano at an officers' cocktail party, where he performed so well that it became his permanent assignment for the duration. He was even given a special uniform so that he would not look like a plain private. He was given his own table, with the very best steaks and the customary bottle of wine. And when he returned from the war, he had made the transition from the classics to the new mood of the bubbly, giddy twenties—light operettas, musicals, dance tunes, Jazz Age jazz: "Yes, We Have No Bananas," "Barney Google," "I Want to Be Happy." Ray Kroc played them with zest, bouncing on his piano stool.

Back in Chicago, he put in a short stint as a board marker for a downtown stockbroker. Then he began picking up odd bookings with orchestras and small bands and finally the best, like Isham Jones and Harry Sosnick, who had the orchestra at the A & P Carnival. Soon he was making $150 a week but by 1922 he had married his first wife, and something about his life did not agree with the puritan streak in him.

Ray Kroc would subsequently point out that the Bohemians are really a very conservative people. He disapproved of the kind of life musicians lived—working nights and sleeping days, irregular meals and occasional barroom rowdiness, too much drinking and too many shady ladies.

Ray Kroc quit the big bands and turned to his second love. He turned to selling, hiring on with a big paper-cup firm, Lily-Tulip, founded some time earlier by a German baroness who had been appalled that a typhoid epidemic among New York schoolchildren had been traced to a single tin cup from which everybody drank. The paper-cup industry, however, quickly found itself even better adapted to the field of fast food and in-plant feeding. And though Ray Kroc did not know it then, when he filled his sample case with Lily-Tulip paper cups, he was launched on the path of his fortune in food.

From the ashes of World War I, some twenty thousand new

American millionaires would spring into being. Kroc's faith was shared by millions of Americans during the twenties. The rush of American progress inspired everybody to think big. The Model T and the radio were transforming the country. The first radio broadcast—the returns of the Harding-Cox election—had been made in 1920 by a one-hundred-watt transmitter in Philadelphia. Two years later there were only twenty-two radio stations in the whole country—by 1929, however, there would be more than fifty in Chicago alone.

Ray Kroc's introduction to radio came when the medium still consisted of crystal sets and headphones, but he was excited by the potential. It was something to get in on, on the ground floor, and not long after landing his job with Lily-Tulip and the birth of his daughter, he found a second job at Chicago's pioneer radio station, WGES, playing the piano, arranging the music programs, and accompanying the singers.

Ray Kroc believed in the bounty of America and the free-enterprise system. He believed in opportunities, and in the twenties the Age of Opportunity had dawned. A man sat in the White House who would remain one of Ray Kroc's lifelong heroes. The President's initials, it was pointed out by his admirers, were the same as those of "Chamber of Commerce." They also spelled out the pervasive mood of the times, "Coolidge Confidence"; and it was from Calvin Coolidge that Ray Kroc borrowed the motto that in later years bedecked his empire—scrolled, framed and hung on the walls of Hamburger Central, the doors of Hamburger U, in the tiled kitchens of McDonald's and the clubhouse of the San Diego Padres. Entitled "Press On," it read:

> NOTHING IN THE WORLD CAN TAKE
> THE PLACE OF PERSISTENCE.
> TALENT WILL NOT: NOTHING IS
> MORE COMMON THAN UNSUCCESSFUL
> MEN WITH TALENT.
> GENIUS WILL NOT: UNREWARDED

GENIUS IS ALMOST A PROVERB.
EDUCATION WILL NOT: THE WORLD
IS FULL OF EDUCATED DERELICTS.
PERSISTENCE AND DETERMINATION
ALONE ARE OMNIPOTENT.

Shortly after his election in 1924, Calvin Coolidge summed up the spirit that imbued the decade and the marketplace. "After all," he concluded to a large gathering of newspaper editors, "the chief business of the American people is business. They are profoundly concerned with producing, selling, investing and prospering in the world. I am strongly of the opinion that the great majority of the people will always find these are moving impulses of our life." A year later he hailed American business as "one of the great contributing forces to the moral and spiritual advancement of the human race."

With the blessing of Coolidge, the passion for wealth became a national obsession. Thus the twenties were a time of huge waves of mergers and a skyrocketing stock market. Business boomed as never before. Eldorado had been found, and it was on Wall Street. Everybody took a flyer. Everybody could clean up by working hard and investing in the market, by buying a piece of real estate, by snatching opportunity. Everybody could be rich. "Everybody Ought to Be Rich," wrote the vice-president of General Motors in the *Ladies' Home Journal.*

Ray Kroc's first opportunity came along at WGES one day in the form of two homely-looking white vaudeville performers by the name of Correll and Gosden. A song-and-patter team, they did a little shuffle and joked and sang, and Ray Kroc signed them on for five dollars a night apiece. At the same time he hired another duo, Tom Malley and Little Jack Little, also for five dollars a night.

Now, Ray Kroc really liked Malley and Little Jack Little. He thought they were funny, and they could also sing and dance. But he did not like Correll and Gosden at all. Neither could carry a note, they weren't funny, and they couldn't dance. After a few nights he advised them to get some material. "You just haven't got it," he told them.

Correll and Gosden took Ray Kroc's advice. After another brief stint as Sam and Henry, they got some new material, which they delivered in an overwrought, mocking black dialect. Raymond Gosden called himself "Amos"; Correll, with the deeper voice, was "Andy."

Astoundingly enough, they were an overnight success, and soon the country would stand still when Amos and Andy came on the air, as would Ray Kroc—to reflect on the fickleness of "opportunity" and the twists and turns of "timing."

Success in the twenties, like prosperity a decade later, was always just around the corner. In 1925 the Florida land boom was on, sending shock waves of new hope through the country. When the land boom reached its peak in the fall, it had exceeded any other gold rush or business stampede in U.S. history. Back in Chicago, Ray Kroc remembered his father's words and joined the trek along the abominable Dixie Highway to Florida, driving down with his wife and baby daughter in a brand-new Model T that didn't have one of the original tires on it when they finally reached Fort Lauderdale.

But once again opportunity proved fickle. The company he went to work for was one of the biggest in the Florida real estate business. It owned twenty-two Hudson sedans, each limousine with its own chauffeur. Ray Kroc formed part of the company's crack team of salesmen who each day toured buyers around in the chauffeured sedans. He was selling land like hot cakes and sang the praises of Florida as "a fantasy for somebody up north." His commissions were piling up. His sales magic worked wonders. He grew lyrical. Each spiel was a paean to the future of Florida and the opportunities for investment.

But he didn't see any money. The properties he sold consisted of a whole lot of swamp and a little bit of dirt—low land grown over with mangrove trees. And when the prospective buyers got home they inevitably had second thoughts. None of the deals was being closed. The northern banks quit lending money to the real estate companies. The bubble burst, and thousands of spielers like Ray Kroc were stuck, with no way home.

Ray Kroc's luck stayed down until 1926. He was broke, but he landed a job as a piano player with Willard Robinson and his Deep-River Boys on Palm Island. They played in a speakeasy called the Silent Night, one of the swankiest places in Florida. It boasted a pagoda, a marble dance floor surrounded by Grecian columns, tuxedoed waiters, exquisite landscaping, a three-hundred-foot yacht, tropical shrubs, and an eight-foot-high barbed-wire fence complete with lookout and a buzzer in case the Revenuers came.

Prohibition was in force, and at the Silent Night people did their drinking on the yacht, which was owned by a rum-runner whom everyone knew only as "Doc." Doc had floodlights out on the water in case the Revenuers came by boat, and his own high-speed launch that he used to run between Palm Island and Bimini with cargoes of booze. He kept the bottles in a black burlap bag in the water, pulling them out with a hook, while the patrons kept their bottles on the railing so they could easily dump the evidence overboard in case of an unexpected visit by federal agents.

Ray Kroc tinkled away at the piano for a while, but never really became one of the Deep-River Boys. After replenishing his cash, he sent his wife and daughter back to Chicago by train and drove the Model T back himself. He arrived in Chicago in a snowstorm, without an overcoat, huddled in his battered car. A few days later he was back on the road again with his sample case of Lily-Tulip paper cups.

Kroc was in bad financial shape, but hardly disillusioned. And because his faith never wavered, he returned to Fort Lauderdale a half century later in his own $4.5 million jet—to his own magnificent white mansion with a doorbell that

chimed merrily, tinkling over what used to be a whole lot of
swamp and a little bit of dirt.

"You Deserve a Break Today," it chimes.

Ray Albert Kroc never lost the Coolidge Confidence—unlike
"Cal, Our Pal," who wisely announced that he would not run
in 1928. The Crash came the following year, ending the myth
of the twenties.

Just before the stock market collapsed, at the height of the
boom, 60 percent of all Americans earned less than $2,000
a year, the bare minimum for the basic necessities of life.
The boom itself had been fed with rigged deals, insider
trading, and overpriced stock. The banks, the instruments of
all the flimflam, began bolting their doors. The giant new
business wonders collapsed into a rubble of empty shells, and
as their directors retreated in dignified silence, Americans
began standing in line for bread and soup, for charity and
jobs, for the elusive chicken in every pot.

Amid the gloom of the depression, Kroc stopped playing
music altogether. He concentrated on his paper-cup route and
sang the praises of Lily-Tulip, and as salesman he must have
been a nonpareil. Nobody could touch him. He knew jokes and
baseball stories, had the salesman's knack for small talk, was
sharp but never offensive. And because he seemed to unre-
servedly believe in everything he sold, he was prone to great
enthusiasms. After a few years of Lily-Tulip he had worked
himself up to Midwest sales manager, but in 1937, when a half
million American workers sat down on their jobs and fascism
raged in Europe and China, Ray Kroc was through selling
paper cups. He had apparently been seized by a great
enthusiasm and a devotion that would last through the next
two decades.

The object of his excitement was a strange metal contraption
with six gleaming prongs. When plugged in, the prongs
rotated at high speed like six frantic eggbeaters. An old friend,

Earl Prince of the Prince Castle Ice Cream stores, demonstrated the gadget, a simple electrical appliance that could make six milk shakes at the same time. For Ray Kroc it was love at first sight. He quickly made a deal with Prince and became the world's exclusive sales agent for the Prince Castle Multi-Mixer.

Many years later, the Hamburger King would mark his shift to the Multi-Mixer business as "the beginning of paying the price"—or more lugubriously, "the sacrifice payable in blood." His quest for business independence began with a ransom—the sum of $85,000 payable to the president of the Lily-Tulip paper-cup firm to be relieved from a work contract on which he owed two more years. He borrowed the money, and for the first two years of selling Multi-Mixers he was broke and in debt. He lived on "mortgage hill" and bought his Ford on time.

Ray Kroc's travels provided him with a first-hand education in the restaurant business, taking him to all types of eating establishments. He had called on White Castle and White Tower, the last bastions of the nickel hamburger people were urged to buy "by the sack"; and he carried his products not just to restaurants and chain operations but to places like Chicago's Coliseum, the Amphitheatre, the Cubs ball park and in-plant feeding concessionaires—and, farther afield, to smaller outfits like Rocky Built in Denver and Little Taverns in Washington, D.C. Later, when his Multi-Mixer beat took him mostly to ice-cream stands, he learned that phase of the business, too. He sold to Dairy Queen, Dari Delight, Tastee Freez, Friendly Ice Cream—all the ice-cream stores and soft-ice-cream stands. He even developed a line of ice cream—a "wonderful item for bars"—in a champagne glass doused with liqueur, which he gave the grandiose name of "Delacato."

While visiting all the different types of food dispensers, Ray

Kroc often looked into the kitchens, where he saw the problems of a fragmented trade with unharnessed potentials. There was inefficiency, waste and temperamental cooks, sloppy service and food whose quality was never consistent. What was needed was a simple product that moved from start to completion in a streamlined path.

He had contemplated hot dogs, then rejected the idea. There were too many kinds of hot dogs—hot dogs with cereal and flour, the all-meat hot dog which is all kinds of meat, the all-beef hot dog, the kosher hot dog. And along with the different varieties, there were all sorts of different ways of cooking hot dogs. They could be boiled, broiled, rotisseried, charcoaled and on and on. Hamburgers, on the other hand, were simplicity itself. The condiments were added to the hamburger, not built in. And there was only one way to prepare the hamburger—to grill it. Then you served it with french fries and you had a basic menu that lent itself to step-by-step control.

To Ray Kroc the key to a revolution in the restaurant trade was simplicity and so hamburgers and french fries seem to have remained in the back of his mind all through the depression, Pearl Harbor, Hiroshima, the postwar boom, and Korea. In the meantime, his affairs prospered, though modestly. Over the years he grew blockier, more compact. He kept his blond hair brilliantined, slick and shiny. He wore a bow tie and roomy suits. He played bridge and could even afford to join a modest country club. He acquired a nice home in Arlington Heights, one of Chicago's better suburbs, and like most middle-class Americans he lived comfortably along prescribed markers of status. Then, in 1954, he met the McDonalds. Ray Kroc was fifty-two years old.

The meeting came at a fretful moment, a time when he was growing increasingly restless. He was past what he considered his prime. Those indispensable factors of fortune, opportunity and timing, appeared to be moving steadily out of reach. "I expect money like you walk into a room and turn on a light switch or a faucet," he confided. "It's not enough." Big money, the kind of money he desired, had always proven elusive, and it was an order for eight Multi-Mixers from the McDonald brothers that finally stung him into reckless, almost desperate action. The brothers ran a hamburger stand in San Bernardino, a town fifty-five miles east of Los Angeles that the locals called San Berdoo. Ray Kroc showed up there one day after deciding that he wanted a firsthand look at an operation that found it necessary to make forty-eight milkshakes at the same time.

The town's distinction was its location as the terminus of the transcontinental Route 66. If not altogether new, it was a new kind of town, of which there were hundreds in southern California and the Southwest. It was inhabited by freeway dwellers in cheap stucco houses. The new gleaming roads swept past them, through vast spaces of desert and oases of irrigated orange groves. The freeway dwellers were motorized as no other section of the population, and had given rise to cults of motorcycle gangs, hotrodders, mechanical shamans, and desolate beer bars. Indeed, the town would be the birthplace of the Hell's Angels.

When Ray Kroc arrived in San Berdoo, the town showed the effects of the postwar transformation that was taking place throughout southern California. Full employment in the war industries had ignited the region's explosive growth, with vast housing tracts, shopping centers, and industries; with highways, ramps, and forests of bright, baked real estate—a prototype of the grid that would cover much of the rest of the country in a few short years. An endless caravan of chrome-laden automobiles trucked the road, so San Berdoo was drive-in country, laced with freeways, gas pumps, eats, and garish eye-popping signs that could be seen from a far distance. It was the sign that directed Ray Kroc to the McDonald's hamburger stand: two radiant arches blazing quietly in the hot sun.

But what struck the Chicago visitor even more as he drew closer were the people that flocked beneath them. All through the day he watched crowds of customers waiting in line, more people than he had ever seen at a drive-in. At dusk the Golden Arches lit up the sky. The lines never seemed to dwindle. Ray Kroc was overcome and cried out softly to himself that this would go anyplace in the world.

Kroc had arrived at the once-in-a-lifetime juncture of the right man, the right time, and the right product. Wartime rationing and wartime in-plant feeding techniques had helped homogenize the American palate. C rations for the millions of troops in Europe had been the forerunner of fast food, leveling tastebuds for the establishment of a bland national cuisine. And in their own queer, stubborn way, the brothers McDonald, like Henry Ford, had somehow developed the rudiments of the assembly-line hamburger.

The mixer salesman was impressed with all he saw at the McDonald's stand: the value, the speed of service, the elimination of wastefulness, the cleanliness. But one thing especially struck him. There was nothing to steal!

There were no plates, dishes, or choice of condiments. The owners served a standard patty with standard sauce for fifteen cents. The trade moved in and out fast. Nobody had to wait for more than a few minutes. And the french fries always tasted fresh and crispy as they came out from under infrared heat lamps, which the innovative McDonald brothers used to keep french fries warm. Like Ray Kroc, the two had also searched for a food item that was cheap, simple, and the same every day of the year: an item they could sell for fifteen cents and make a profit.

Nonetheless Ray Kroc would later refer to the brothers as "a queer pair." They were a tight-knit, taciturn clan and must have been very different from the ebullient, bubbling salesman. There was the parsimonious bachelor Maurice "Mac" McDonald, and Richard McDonald, who was married but had no children. They had come from New Hampshire to California in 1928 to seek their fortune in the Hollywood movie industry. For two dour, dutiful New Englanders this choice was as bizarre as their later predilection for expensive automobiles and the extravagant symbol of the Golden Arches. But Hollywood proved disappointing, and they ended up instead with a movie theater in Glendora, California, which they sold in 1940 to open a hamburger stand in nearby Pasadena. Mac and Dick McDonald ran a tight ship, and eight years later they had worked out the formula for the self-service hamburger stand in San Bernardino, complete with the arches.

Finicky and frugal, Dick and Mac apparently believed in waste not, want not, and had a fetish for cleanliness. Their place was spotless. Their toilet sparkled. Like Ray Kroc later, they seem to have had an antipathy toward teen-agers, who generally tended to hang out, be noisy, and mess up the place. It was to eliminate the teen-age problem that they had decided to convert to self-service. The formula worked and attracted immediate attention.

Well before Ray Kroc's arrival, other would-be entrepreneurs had marveled at the McDonald's operation in San Berdoo, and over the years Dick and Mac McDonald had cautiously sold six other franchises in California. Just before Kroc appeared, they had quietly passed up a deal involving a big chain-type expansion. They were conservative and suspicious of fast deals and not the least worried that others might get richer from their name than they. Dick, his wife, and his perennial bachelor brother, Mac, had a house on a nearby hill with a lovely view, rocking chairs, and three Cadillacs. They were clearing $75,000 a year from their hamburger stand, and they were fearful of thinking *too* big.

Ray Kroc says he stayed in San Bernardino two or three days. He studied the operation carefully, hanging out at the stand from morning till night. He estimated that the single stand was doing $250,000 a year. On the second day he asked the McDonald brothers what kind of deal he could make if he got out and licensed people to open up a McDonald's.

He told them that they had a great idea in fast-food merchandizing, but neither brother appeared very interested. Perhaps they had been wary of the cocky, energetic salesman from the start, and seemed leery of his enthusiasm. Not given to displays of emotion, they listened and continued flipping burgers behind the grill. Then, according to Ray Kroc, Dick McDonald took the visitor's arm. "See that house up there?" he said. "That's home to me and I like it there. If we opened a chain I'd never be home."

But the salesman was adroit at handling such situations. Kroc simply played deaf and kept talking. His nasal midwestern rasp followed them into their tiled hamburger kitchen. It rang through their home on the hill and sawed away at their resistance. Like Cal Coolidge, the salesman pressed on. He proposed that he would go out and sell McDonald's franchises and that, for their part, all the brothers had to do was stay in San Bernardino—in their home on the hill with its lovely view, rocking chairs, and trio of Cadillacs. And by the tenth of every month he would send them a check. They wouldn't need to travel. They wouldn't need to do anything. It would be no trouble for them at all, he said.

Behind their grill the brothers wavered, and at last they agreed. But when they signed the papers, Kroc does not remember that either looked very happy. Ray Kroc had wanted 2 percent of all the gross sales of any franchised store. The brothers said 1.9 percent, out of which Kroc also had to pay them 0.5 percent, so he really ended up with only 1.4 percent. But Ray Kroc gained possession of the thing he coveted most—the name.

Ray Kroc returned to Chicago. He thought he had them. But his problems with the McDonalds were just beginning, fought in the classic spirit of free enterprise—with lawyers, threats, clauses, subordinate clauses, fine legal print, and appeals to self-interest. The fight began when the brothers sold the Chicago territory not long after making their deal with him. When Ray Kroc objected that he was supposed to be their exclusive national representative, Dick McDonald laconically replied that he still had the rest of the country. It cost Ray Kroc $25,000 to get Cook County back. He cussed, but he shelled out the money.

However, the chief bone of contention between Kroc and the two brothers in San Berdoo was a provision in the contract that specified he could make no change in the retail store concept without a registered letter from the McDonalds. This stipulation applied even to such items as installing a basement or a furnace. And from the very first, Dick and Mac made it clear that they had no intention of ever sending such a letter. Ray Kroc went to see their attorney, who told him that if the brothers wouldn't write him a letter *he* would be in default for Kroc had already sold dozens of McDonald's franchises. And in every one, the store concept had been modified and changed to suit local conditions. Some had furnaces, some had air conditioning, some had different types of equipment. So for years, as his sale of franchises mounted, so did his fear that one day Dick and Mac would simply squeeze him out of the operation with that loophole. There was nothing to prevent the brothers from declaring him in breach of the agreement and selling the McDonald's name to someone else. Finally, one day in 1960, he called San Bernardino on impulse and asked Dick McDonald to sell him back the contract.

Ray said he wanted everything—the trademarks, copyrights, formulas, the Golden Arches, and, above all, the name. He offered the brothers a half million dollars. Dick and Mac took their time deliberating and then called back. They said he could take it or leave it. The price was $2.7 million.

Ray Kroc received the news in his office in downtown Chicago. He says he dropped the phone. When, on the other end of the line, Dick McDonald innocently asked what the noise was, Ray Kroc replied, "It's me jumping from the twentieth floor of the LaSalle-Wacker Building."

In the end it was not Ray Kroc's flair for drama that garnered the purchase money asked by the brothers. It was a friend from an ice-cream chain, a man fifteen years his junior named Harry J. Sonneborn, who had joined Ray Kroc as a hundred-dollar-a-week partner. A former vice-president of Tastee Freez, Sonneborn was slick and had a keen financial sense. Sonneborn managed to round up a number of college endowment funds that agreed to a five-year loan at an exorbitant annual interest. The $2.7 million ended up costing $14 million, so the fledgling Hamburger King again paid the price. And then he took sweet revenge. In their final deal with him, the McDonald brothers had neglected to mention that they planned to keep their pet store in San Bernardino. But because they could no longer use their own name, the stand was now called Mac's Place. When word of this got back to Chicago, Ray Kroc must have been boiling mad. A few months later, two Golden Arches towered across the road from Mac's Place. It was a hamburger stand. Spotless, red-and-white-tiled. Except for the McDonald's name the hamburger stand was an exact copy of their own, arches and all.

The magic of their own name across the road proved too potent and soon the brothers gave up and moved out of their home on the hill. They returned to the small town of Bedford in New Hampshire, the green, rolling New England country they had left as young men. Mac died in 1972, just a short while after the governor of New Hampshire appeared in nearby Concord with Ray Kroc to open the fifteen-hundredth McDonald's outlet.

The Hamburger King seemed to take deep satisfaction from having finally gotten even with the persnickety brothers. "Whatever it turned out," he would reflect, "that was the price I had to pay in order to own my own business and to develop my own destiny." With Dick and Mac out of the way, the prize was within reach. He had survived the cruelties of the marketplace, and in 1972, during an interview with the food service magazine *Institutions,* Kroc expressed the wisdom of the "self-made" experience.

"Look, it is ridiculous to call this an industry," he explained. "This is not. This is rat eat rat, dog eat dog. I'll kill 'em, and I'm going to kill 'em before they kill me. You're talking about the American way of survival of the fittest."

In the Beginning

"Grinding It Out"

A few months after he had first returned from southern California with the McDonald's agreement, Ray Kroc opened his first stand, in Des Plaines, near Chicago. The store had the standard exterior—the red-and-white-tile front, the Golden Arches, and the name. Kroc put up his own money for this prototype, hiring a manager by the name of Ed Mac-Luckie to run it. Some time later he sold his first actual franchise, in Fresno, California; and soon another, in Reseda, California. Kroc's first franchise in Fresno would garner millions with a total of six stands. Then the busy salesman cast about for a young fellow to help him with the day-to-day business chores.

Kroc's hiring policies were based on his own firm standards. "First it was the will and the strong back, hard work and perseverance," he said, "a guy who loves what he's doing and goes at it with verve and spirit and a desire and enthusiasm." It was his oft-quoted dictum that if a person possessed these qualities, he couldn't care less about "the I.Q." And the young man fitting these requisites of dedication and hard work was already standing behind the grill in the very first McDonald's in Des Plaines. Baby-faced at twenty-three, fresh from Des Moines, an abortive spell at rural Drake College, and a hitch in the military, Fred Turner was standing there intently flipping hamburgers when his boss took him aside. Turner's was a face that could have been minted from the crowd, its regular, unspectacular features ill-fitted to any expression other than total seriousness. It betrayed a personality that was perhaps not too lively but it also showed the spotless sterling that could be relied on: a character that was loyal and doggedly insistent on getting things done to the satisfaction of the boss.

When Fred Turner, newly married and just back from Korean War service, found a job at the Des Plaines hamburger stand, he was not very different from the millions of other young husbands and veterans seeking a livelihood in the fearful era of the Red scare witch-hunts and cold-war spy mania. They struggled for their niche in a period of ever-diminishing opportunities for the vaunted self-made American, the self-reliant merchant charting his own course to financial security. In this constricting climate, franchising was widely hailed as the last frontier of the independent businessman, and up until Kroc singled him out, it had been the sum of Fred Turner's ambition to acquire one day his own hamburger franchise from McDonald's. But after listening to his boss, Fred Turner abandoned his initial goal and joined the fledgling McDonald's Corporation.

Despite his youth, Fred Turner was given large responsibilities. While Kroc stayed on the road selling licenses, Turner was to oversee the company's daily operation. The total number of stands still numbered less than a half dozen, but Kroc's vision was large, and Fred grabbed the chance to grow with the vision.

For Ray Kroc could foresee the day when the assembly-line

hamburger would embrace nothing less than a "System"—a patty-to-patron production line spanning a network of suppliers, truckers, and outlets. He predicted that one day this "System" would cover the country, requiring specially trained cadres of managers, assistant managers, crew personnel, field inspectors, regional and area supervisors: a crack corps in white shirts and crew hats to man thousands of stands from coast to coast. He assigned to Turner the task of training and molding the ranks of the franchisees who signed up to carry the McDonald's name and abide by the "Formula." "There is a science to making and serving a hamburger," he instructed his young protégé.

Fred Turner studied the Science, which was expressed by what looked to be at first two impossible anagrams, "QSC/TLC." Ray Kroc explained their meaning: *"Quality Service Cleanliness/Tender Loving Care."* He then charged Fred with the special mission of spreading this message to all the new licensees, the grill- and countermen, the managers and kitchen crews. Not just to spread it like lip service, but to drill it home. And Fred Turner did, with extraordinary, irrepressible, indefatigable zeal.

The first McDonald's stands exhibited QSC/TLC and the founder's bedrock fast-food fundamentals: a clean, well-lighted place, devoid of jukeboxes, cigarette machines, pinball machines, or vending devices of any kind. "Our theme," Ray Kroc was fond of repeating, "is kind of synonymous with Sunday school, the Girl Scouts, and the YMCA. McDonald's is clean and wholesome."

Sharing the popular view of the fifties, which portrayed adolescents as a grave social menace, he did everything to keep teen-agers from loitering about, even going so far as to initially ban all young female employees because "they attracted the wrong kind of boys."

At McDonald's there were to be no telephone booths or newsstands or posters in the window. No gum on the floor, no cigarette butts or papers littering the lot. In the kitchens there would be none of that galvanized, tin, junky stuff. Everything was to be stainless steel. The windows had to be washed inside and out every day. All employees were to observe strict grooming standards—clean nails, short hair, shiny black shoes. They were to be schooled in "please" and "thank you" and "have a nice day." Every McDonald's had to look bright and sparkling and, one thing above all, the rest rooms had to be spotless. For Ray Kroc apparently knew from his own extensive commercial travels that an immaculate privy was a roadside phenomenon, sought after as much as gas and food. The brisk, happy rumble of good clean plumbing in a spotless white-tiled cubicle, would rank high in the esteem of the suburban middle class that he targeted as McDonald's primary market. Like hamburger and french fries, clean toilets were something basic and simple that everyone could understand. "You wouldn't hire a guy from Harvard?" someone asked Ray Kroc not long ago. And the founder answered, "I *couldn't* hire a guy from Harvard because the son of a bitch wouldn't get down and wash the toilets." But in Fred Turner he found an early disciple who shared all of his ideals and he rewarded the young man with loyalty and promotions. In 1956, after six months of training operators and still a baby-faced twenty-three, he became a full-fledged department head. In 1958 Turner would be vice-president; in 1967, executive vice-president; a year later, president and chief administrative officer; in December, 1973, Ray Kroc would name Turner chief executive officer, the company's highest post. The Hamburger King guided his career and grew to love him almost like a son.

While Fred Turner occupied himself with the affairs of the company, Ray Kroc at advanced middle age exploded with energy. He was back on the road, but there was a new spring to his feet. The going was slow at first at the turn of the mid-fifties. For a while he continued selling his mixers along with McDonald's licenses. Prospects had to be won over, sold on the idea. Steady suppliers had to be established: meat-packers to provide the patties, purveyors for the paper goods and equipment, shortening, buns, cleaning solvents, and so on. Rigid standardization was to be enforced. It all came down to dollars and cents and profits that mounted as the network grew tighter under the more stringent control.

Kroc aggressively pursued new business, concentrating on the growing leisure market. When he heard that his friend Walt Disney was going to open the prettiest, costliest, and most breathtaking amusement park in the world, he called up and asked if he could put one of his hamburger stands there.

Disney invited him to see the vice-president in charge of food and beverages. But when Ray Kroc got to California, he found that Disney had big investors lined up—flush outfits like Carnation Milk and oil companies that could afford to put up big front money for good locations amid the fantastic props of Disneyland. Kroc did not stay long. He and Walt had irreconcilable differences on the subject of french fries, with the father of Mickey Mouse suggesting that, instead of charging ten cents, McDonald's charge fifteen cents and kick back a nickel on every bag. It was one of Ray Kroc's fond aphorisms that McDonald's was "for the needy, not the greedy."

He refused Disney's offer because he considered the fifteen-cent hamburger and the ten-cent bag of french fries an axiomatic part of the Formula, a quick "value" identification like the nickel cigar and the dime cup of coffee. He looked up to Sears and Ford, who had merchandized "value," and he resisted any change in the price of McDonald's basic hamburger as late as 1967, when it was finally raised to eighteen cents.

Besides, the big-profit item was not the hamburger but the crisp golden sticks Ray Kroc called "the greatest french fries in the world." More than hamburgers, "Mac Fries" were his special pride and joy. They were the result of a special process that he himself developed. He called them "Potatoes Raymond."

Ray Kroc took personal charge of the project, which began

by lugging hundred-pound sacks of potatoes—the finest Idaho baking potatoes, the chairman said proudly, that had had Tender Loving Care for about a month, curing at seventy degrees to balance the starches and sugar. Next Kroc personally cut off the bald spots and put the potatoes through a cutting machine to slice them into strips; then they were washed to get the extra starch off; followed by blanching, the first stage of cooking; and then letting them set until cool. It was the final stage that he enjoyed most, watching the pale starchy sticks sink into the fryer, where they bubbled and soon turned a golden brown.

The Potato Raymond represented just one of the many refinements Ray Kroc introduced to the model of the fast-food production line devised by the McDonald brothers. Each innovation made the menu and service more uniform; each refinement served the cause of standardization, volume, and profit. Speed, as formulated by the founder and taught by Fred Turner, constituted the essence of Hamburger Science. After timing the operation, Ray Kroc allotted 50 seconds to serve a hamburger, shake, and french fries. Further breakthroughs added to the propulsion of profits. A milestone was achieved in 1959, when a record thirty-six hamburgers were served in 110 seconds.

Speed of service depended to a large extent on the uniformity of menu items, and Kroc boasted that he had worked out the precise formula for making a hamburger to the public's liking. This basic machine-cut hamburger patty weighed 1.6 ounces, measured 3.875 inches in diameter, and contained no lungs, hearts, cereal, or soybeans. In each pound of meat there were ten hamburgers, which were to contain no more than 19 percent fat. Everything was calculated, down to the exact size of the bun (3½ inches wide) and the amount of onions that went on it (one-fourth of an ounce). In addition, the bun had to have a higher-than-normal sugar content for faster browning. It was also determined that french fries were to be thrown away if they were seven minutes old, hamburgers after ten minutes, coffee after thirty—which were the times they turned stale. In later years McDonald's headquarters, popularly known as Hamburger Central, would even lay down precise specifications concerning the amount of food each unit was expected to throw away.

Ray Kroc formulated the nationwide operating policies. No detail seemed too small for his ever-vigilant eye. The outward appearance of the stands scrupulously maintained the red-and-white-tile fronts. The largest sign-maker in Indiana was engaged to embellish the arches, and one of the early primitive eye-stoppers showed a giant arch surmounted by a hamburger in the shape of a figure brandishing a ladle, and beneath it the legend:

> Licensee McDonald's
> Speedee Service System
> Hamburgers
> Over 10 Million Sold

The proliferation of the name and the sign was noted as early as 1958: "National Restaurant Association conventioneers are besieging Chicago's Ray Kroc for dope on how he sells hamburgers for fifteen cents and built an eighty store chain operation in three years," reported Chicago *Daily Tribune* columnist Herb Lyon. A year later, Ray Kroc opened the hundredth McDonald's drive-in. Like the golden spike that joined the Union and Pacific Railroads, the ceremony marked a milestone: the Golden Arches ranged from coast to coast. The McDonald's sign straddled a crisscross grid of small and medium-sized towns like Perth Amboy, New Jersey; Lancaster, Pennsylvania; Lewiston, Maine; Roanoke, Virginia; Meriden, Connecticut; Tucson, Arizona; Quincy, Illinois; Terre Haute, Indiana; Yonkers, New York; Columbus, Ohio; and Duluth, Minnesota. There were eleven McDonald's in Florida alone. Twenty were planned for Wisconsin. Kroc's first stand grossed $158,000 in its first year of operations, but by 1959 the gross per site had risen to a $204,000 average. Fifty million hamburgers had been sold, and the founder had his picture taken by Yousuf Karsh of Ottawa, the portrait photographer of Pope John XXIII.

At the start of the sixties, the chairman of the bustling corporation took to the air lanes with the same alacrity that once transported him behind the wheel of his first Model T. The highway no longer served to keep up with McDonald's surging growth. In a leased company plane, Ray Kroc looked down with binoculars through cracks in the clouds, noting church steeples and traffic intersections, tangents of substantial family neighborhoods, shopping centers. From the air he charted his capture of the suburbs, which meant children, mothers, businessmen—anyone who was "fussy . . . clean and proud." Figuring, for example, that churchgoers qualified, he counted the steeples.

Until McDonald's came upon the scene, most of the large restaurant chains stuck close to the urban core. Vintage names like Horn and Hardart and White Castle were to be found mainly in downtown areas. But, flying through the clouds, Ray Kroc could see a vast population shift taking place. Tricycles and bicycles on neat lawns, garages with one car and space for two, mushrooming housing tracts filled with happy consumers— the people with chunks of "disposable income."

But while the chairman surveyed the suburbs from the air, the decisive action took place on the ground. It was then led by Kroc's partner, Harry Sonneborn, the former executive of Tastee Freez, who was busy transforming McDonald's from a struggling, chugging chain into a pounding patty piston, powering a mighty McMoney Machine. It was Sonneborn who got Ray Kroc out of what was ruefully called the "franchising bind."

The franchising bind had been implicit in the contract Ray Kroc signed with the McDonald brothers. Its most severe constriction was the 1.9 percent-of-profits license fee—which was all he could charge franchisees for purchasing the McDonald's name and formula. The "franchising bind" quickly proved to be an instrument of financial torture, keeping Kroc's profits low. In 1960, after selling nearly two hundred licenses doing an annual business of $37 million, his own *gross* franchise income over the years amounted to a lackluster $700,000—virtually all of which he plowed back or paid in fees to the original licensors, the brothers McDonald in San Berdoo. His income during this period was so little, in fact, that the chairman was forced to subsist on the sale of his Prince Castle mixing marvels.

Harry Sonneborn apparently realized that the license fee would have to be supplemented by other sources of income. He found it in land and rentals, and the plan he worked out made the annual license fee subsidiary to a far heftier levy. In effect, the plan took McDonald's into the real estate business. Sonneborn made McDonald's into a landlord. The company selected the site, built the store, filled it with equipment, and rented the package to an operator, who would thus be both licensee *and* tenant. The franchisee paid a rental fee based on his annual revenues—along with the annual service charge and a one-shot license payment.

The immediate investment required to launch Sonneborn's plan was $1.5 million, a sum he managed to round up after Ray Kroc had been turned down by several banks. Sonneborn obtained the loan at a stiff rate from several New England insurance firms, which agreed to put up the money for 22½ percent of McDonald's, a chunk of stock that would be worth some $500 million a decade later.

Ironically, as success seemed to draw nearer, Kroc's ownership of McDonald's dwindled. Besides the 22½ percent that went to the insurance firms, he gave 10 percent of McDonald's to his secretary as stock in lieu of salary. Additional blocks of stock had gone to Sonneborn and others among his early associates—so that by the time Kroc had disposed of the McDonald brothers and freed himself from the "franchising bind," he was down to owning just about half of the company he had founded.

But at the same time the dragons of greedy bankers and hungry competitors that stood in the way of the free-enterprise treasure had been slain. With the added spur of increased fees and rents from McDonald's license-holders, Kroc was getting closer to the big buck.

Ray Kroc was sixty years old, and he had the concept, the name, the System, and the real estate to power this money machine. Cheap labor was the fuel, igniting the company's soaring growth. Everything McDonald's earned, the chairman poured back in. With Sonneborn he would anticipate the next three months' profits and obligate them in the way of debt for expansion. The Formula worked beyond their wildest expectations—simple food, quick service, stiff franchise fees, cheap labor, a huge outer real estate ring, and a string of faithful suppliers. The suppliers in particular, strategically located throughout the United States, were to become a key part of Kroc's success.

Like the company's early burger barons who snapped up territorial licenses to plant as many as twenty stands in one area, the provisioners that supplied Kroc's merchandizing machine also grew with McDonald's. They had trust and confidence in his System from the beginning and stood by him through the years. One of Kroc's oldest friends is Lew Perlman of the Martin Brower Corporation, McDonald's paper and sundry supplier, who usually gives the welcoming speech to students on opening day at Hamburger University. Another loyal retainer is Harry Smorgan, who has poured tons of shortening into the patty production gears. There is also Harold Freund of Los Angeles, the world's biggest baker of hamburger buns, and there is Jack Simplot, Idaho's "Potato King."

The affairs of Bill Moore, another old friend of Kroc's, have been equally prosperous. Since 1955 his Los Angeles–based Golden State Foods Corporation has grown into a giant $66 million brokerage house dealing in everything from Coke syrup and frozen patties to a new experimental development which, if successful, will give his company a network for distributing over $1 million in Big Mac sauce alone. Moore's fifty-four delivery trucks link his Golden State Foods to the Golden Arches from Florida to Arizona, to California and Alaska, and handle shipments to Hawaii and to the *largest* single McDonald's stand in Guam.

Ray Kroc's own Prince Castle Company, of Multi-Mixer fame, was sold and turned up as a division of Martin Brower. Prince Castle supplied McDonald's franchisees and company-run stores with a continual stream of updated gadgets and parts, from catsup dispensers to bun boards. Like Martin Brower and Golden State Foods, Prince Castle constantly ranked as an "approved supplier," designated as such by McDonald's.

With only 250 stands, McDonald's was already noted as a giant in the fast-food industry. Kilt-clad bagpipers appeared in shopping plazas in the Midwest, drumming up the "thrifffttteee" aspect of McDonald's "amazing menu." Newspapers reported incredulously that customers at McDonald's "could eat off the floor." In 1960 McDonald's published statistics showing that Americans each chomped 2.95 hamburgers a week. The Cleveland *Properties* headlined: "The Mighty Hamburger Makes a Lot of Cabbage."

The success of the System snowballed. In 1962 total sales soared to over $76 million. A year later the company unveiled an important new item: the double burger and double cheeseburger. Another fast-food model saw the light in 1964, Filet-O-Fish. In that same year McDonald's noted that it had sold a total of over 400 million hamburgers, 120 million pounds of french fries, and 400 billion slices of pickle. The mayor of Gary, Indiana, declared a Hamburger Day, and in Madison, Wisconsin, students vied to win the newly established $200 McDonald's Citizenship Award.

Planted in the thick of American life, at crossroads and busy neighborhood intersections, McDonald's reflected the current

of trends and events. In Addison, Illinois, not far from the
company's future headquarters, it opened its own research lab
to develop and test new items of kitchen equipment. Civil
rights demonstrators succeeded in desegregating a McDonald's
stand in Pine Bluff, Arkansas. And at the onset of Beatlemania,
the company banned all moptops for its employees. "With the
Beatle haircut, their caps don't fit their heads," explained the
urgent directive to all franchisees, managers, and operators.
At the end of the hectic year, taking a respite from the frantic
pace, Ray Kroc climbed aboard the M.S. *Gripsholm* for a trip
across the Atlantic with his new wife and a group of friends
from the Des Plaines area, where he had opened his first
franchise.

The triumphal expansion continued the following year. By
the end of 1965 there were 710 McDonald's in forty-four
states, with over 20,000 employees. Plans were announced to
open 100 new stands in Canada, Puerto Rico, and the Virgin
Islands. In the spring the name festooned the Board on Wall
Street and the stock shot up.

In 1966 McDonald's became a national name. It was voted
"the growth company of the year." Its Hamburger University
training center was featured in *Life* magazine with the photo-
graph of a round-faced "professor" quoted in the caption as
saying that "a perfect bun is a beautiful thing." The company
launched its first big national advertising campaign, and about
10 million youngsters entered a contest to choose the riders
on McDonald's floats in Macy's Thanksgiving Day Parade. A
year later McDonald's did $266 million worth of business. Ray
Kroc's share came to $50.5 million. Indeed, he told a San Diego
paper that he was no longer working for money—he was
working "for kicks." He had captured the big buck, the American dream, and he began writing it all down in his planned
autobiography, *Grinding It Out*.

Ray Kroc's achievements are not to be underestimated.
His optimism and faith had nurtured a giant complex. He had
taken meat and potatoes and created a mass menu to fit the

pace of highly industrialized life. He could claim his place among America's mass-merchandizers who had revolutionized the methods of distribution. But above and beyond all this, he was the "All-Time Mr. McDonald's." The farflung hamburger empire had been created by a tireless, unstoppable salesman. With single-minded force, Ray Kroc had sustained McDonald's growth and forged the links of business and sentiment that held the chain together. He had been synthesizer, organizer, impresario, and cheerleader. And even after he moved to the sidelines he never stopped.

As a virtuoso of the sales spiel, Kroc's biggest asset had been an ability to inspire others and get them moving. His success was a complex web of contributions made by people whom he had been able to charge up with his promise of financial success. At Hamburger Central, legend attributes to the chairman uncanny abilities in picking people. Notwithstanding that the people who praise Kroc for this talent are those who have been selected by him, McDonald's success was due in large part to Kroc's choice of lieutenants. But he had shown an even more necessary quality that enabled him to get rid of the people with the useful talents when they were no longer useful and became a drag on the corporation.

The McDonalds had provided Kroc with the fast-food model—the assembly-line hamburger—and when they became obstacles they vanished from the scene. A similar end befell his other business guru, former partner Harry Sonneborn, whose real estate goose would eventually lay more than half of the company's golden profits. After Sonneborn became a millionaire in 1965, the shrewd financial man apparently began slowing down. He spent more time at home in Alabama and found a consuming hobby in the acquisition of famous autographs—an illustrious collection that reportedly included the signatures of Adolf Hitler and Hermann Göring.

Ray Kroc recalls having had in 1968 a talk with Harry Sonneborn, then the president of McDonald's. "You're not watching the business," he says he told him. "You're not taking care of it like you used to. You're neglecting it. You're gone sometimes two, three weeks at a time. You're going to have to move over, Harry."

They had a signed agreement, and Sonneborn, as Kroc remembers it, said, "Not me. I'm in the contract."

"Look," Kroc said, employing the same tactic that had eliminated the brothers McDonald, "I'll make an offer that you can't turn down because you're too smart."

For $100,000 a year for the rest of his life, Harry Sonneborn submitted his resignation, taking his own large chunk of McDonald's stock with him. But when he finally walked out, his farewell to the Hamburger Empire was apparently bitter.

Hamburger King Ray Kroc would only glower as he remembered the end of the whole Sonneborn affair: . . . "Harry became vindictive and traded all his McDonald's stock in for Blue Chip: Penn Railroad, U.S. Steel, A.T. & T., Union Carbide. . . ."

3

Hamburger Central

"I Wanted to Be Sure We Didn't Build a Monster"

Hamburger Central (as insiders call it) rises eight stories high. The lobby is lined with banks of dull-black elevators. The space vaults high on granite pillars that dwarf the receptionist at her desk. Wearing a blue blazer with the crossed-arches logo on her bosom, she smiles stiffly at the windswept emptiness of McDonald's Plaza.

When McDonald's decided to build a new headquarters, the edifice was designed to blend in with its location in Oak Brook, a modern corporate oasis out in Chicago's western suburbs. The lower five floors were leased to a variety of tenants, while McDonald's staked out its preserve on the upper three. This became the heart of the hamburger empire.

McDonald's move from Chicago's crowded Loop to Hamburger Central in March of 1971 marked a new stage in the company's growth. Its new home was hailed as the "tallest office building in the world built on the profits of hamburgers." The size of its new headquarters demonstrated the fact that McDonald's had come of age. The humble burger stand had become big business and had joined its Oak Brook neighbors: giant companies like Sears, Stouffer, 'Armour, and Sheraton. Since the first patty back in 1955, McDonald's had expanded from its single, garish, candy-striped stand into a patty-to-patron production machine that in 1974 sold $2 billion worth of fast food, the average stand doing well over $600,000 in sales.

McDonald's bought 1 percent of all the beef wholesaled in the United States. The billion burgers it sold every four months required that 100,000 head of cattle be fed, slaughtered, processed, frozen into patties, and distributed across the country. Just this mammoth herd alone required the full-time services of 700 cowboys. McDonald's was also the country's biggest buyer of processed potatoes for making french fries and the top purchaser of fish. It was also the nation's leading employer of young people, some 150,000. By 1976 there were thirty-five hundred McDonald's stands, with hundreds slated to be opened during the following year. The company name girdled the globe, a burger belt spanning North and Central America, Europe, Japan, and Australia. McDonald's own research happily forecast that the planet could easily support twelve thousand of its outlets under current conditions.

The formidable complex known as Hamburger Central bore witness to McDonald's reputation as an "authentic" American success story—the small business of selling hamburgers and fries developed into a sophisticated "System." Business periodicals lauded the company for succeeding in a field where 90 percent of the new ventures failed, and held up its achievements as a model for thousands of like-minded small-business hopefuls.

The praise was understandable. In five years alone the company's profits rose by close to 400 percent. Each year it grew by 40 percent, scoring nearly double the sales record of its three closest rivals. A conservative $5,000 invested in McDonald's stock was worth $350,000 in a few short years. Thus, for every 130 million hamburgers sold, the patty-production machine turned out one multimillionaire. In 1972 McDonald's annual profits rose to over $36 million, and one of its shiny new parlors sprang up full-blown somewhere in the country every day of the year. In sales volume McDonald's exceeded its nearest fast-food rival, Colonel Sanders' Kentucky Fried Chicken; in food volume it surpassed the U.S. army, to become America's biggest provider of meals; and at last appropriated to itself the honor of having replaced the hot dog as the national meal.

Perhaps none was more surprised, even puzzled, by Hamburger Central's awesome dimensions than some of McDonald's burger cooks who achieved undreamed-of financial success as the company grew. Fred Turner, for instance, is said to claim to this day that he does not know how McDonald's got this big. But what made Hamburger Central the more remarkable was the fact that, in an era of giant corporate takeovers, McDonald's had been able to avoid all entanglements. In the sixties all of its top rivals were swallowed up by huge food conglomerates—the Burger King chain by Pillsbury, Burger Chef by General Foods, Jack in the Box by Ralston-Purina. But McDonald's remained independent. McDonald's was uniquely Ray Kroc's "baby."

Johnny Carson cracked jokes about it on *The Tonight Show,* Woody Allen and Bob Hope poked fun, Linda Bird Johnson confessed it her favorite food, Tricia Nixon offered it to Prince Charles, Mary Tyler Moore used it on her show.

In less than two decades McDonald's was secure in the American mainstream, a familar tableau of arches, a flag, and garnet sign that proclaimed in gold numbers the total amount of hamburgers sold. This scoreboard changed every four months, as the number was unceremoniously upped by one billion.

The company's headquarters are startling. Behind the arches and the billion-burger sign stands a large bureaucratic apparatus. Like all bureaucracies, it has assumed a life of its own—an independent function to manage, rule, levy, and collect. Hamburger Central's function is this control. Its four massive wings contain a profusion of departments to deal with each and every aspect of McDonald's operations. Central runs nearly a thousand company-owned stores. It plays host to visiting real estate specialists, legal counsel, politicians, security analysts, and tax experts. A prominent area on the seventh floor is bedecked with the flags of nations hosting McDonald's outlets.

Insiders call it the "White Tower." Its formidable appearance is strangely at odds with the notion of McDonald's as a friendly neighborhood kind of place. Carl Kay, a chubby account executive with Cooper and Golin, McDonald's public relations firm, is well aware of it. "The whole McDonald's philosophy is that going to McDonald's is fun, the kind of place where you go to enjoy yourself," says Kay. "People don't think of Hamburger Central and Hamburger University. They think of the McDonald's down the block, and the company prefers to keep it that way."

Nevertheless, the wonders of Hamburger Central have been noted by the outside world. Since its opening, hosts of curious sightseers, reporters, guests, VIPs and industrial designers have come to look and wander through the building. Swedish and German television crews have showed up. A Japanese delegation has paid its respects. In particular, visitors react to the futuristic design. Inside Hamburger Central there are no desks and no walls.

In April, 1969, Chairman Kroc had proudly unveiled the mock-up of the new corporate citadel, featuring a central office tower and four one-story office units topped by Plexiglas domes to admit natural light. But the pride of the place was an octagonal one-story structure in front of the building; called "Ramond's," after the founder, it was to feature a higher-priced luxury hamburger.

Nothing was heard of the mock-up's eventual disposition, and when Hamburger Central finally arose on McDonald's Plaza it bore not the slightest resemblance to the model unveiled by Kroc. There was also no Ramond's, and the chairman would henceforth admit half-apologetically that the new complex "had more Fred Turner in it than me."

Fred Turner, McDonald's daring young president, had hired a "space designer" from Atlanta by the name of William L. Pulgram to thrust the company into the future. Pulgram came up with the "total-concept environment," an office setting that was planned from the landscaping right down to the last piece of furniture. Fred Turner liked the idea, but before going ahead, Pulgram cautiously checked it out with the "experts." "I wanted to be sure we didn't build a monster," he said, "so I touched base with a couple of experimental psychologists and they said it was good."

Space design was in its infancy, and McDonald's offered Pulgram three floors with a total of 33,000 square feet. The result was the "open office," a vastness devoid of obstructions: no walls, and a variety of "work units" that took the place of conventional offices.

Pulgram banished the traditional desk, confining Hamburger Central's four hundred employees instead to Task Response Modules (TRMs) a series of whatnot shelves to house typewriters, writing surfaces, drawing boards, adding machines, and other office paraphernalia. A boxlike palisade of low, burlap-covered cabinets separated these "work units." Seated in his TRM, the occupant found himself marooned in office traffic that inevitably drew him in when he stood up and could suddenly see over his low cabinet enclosure into practically every other such unit.

In order to give adequate play to quirks of personality in the thoroughly planned environment, each Task Response Module came with a bulletin board that the employee could scribble on or festoon with expressions of individual whimsy, simple practical truths such as "It isn't the mountains ahead that wear you out, it's the grain of sand in your shoe." But the most common inspirational message to be found on the TRM walls is Ray Kroc's "Press On" quote from Calvin Coolidge. Others show morale boosters, such as the dollar bill in which George Washington has been replaced by a set of Golden Arches. The "whimsiest" of all the TRM accouterments to be found in the building is a punching bag.

According to Pulgram, the open office was simply a reflection of what was happening in American society today. "We live in an age of individual self-expression—do your own thing. So we have to give individuals enough freedom to put *themselves* in the space we provide."

The spirit unfettered at Hamburger Central sparked even bolder strokes for freedom. Under the slogan, "We play hookey on Friday afternoon, why don't you?" the last day of the work week became known as the "Short and Casual Friday," when employees were permitted to come to the office in golf slacks, shorts, and other forms of leisure wear, skip lunch, and leave early at 1 P.M. Fred Turner noted to his satisfaction that the Short and Casual Friday benefited the productive output. Ray Kroc acknowledged that he would recommend it to every businessman.

One problem soon became clear, however. There was *too* much space, *too* much freedom. And the answer was plants, large potted ferns and shrubs and vines that soon seemed to be creeping everywhere. The remaining gaps in the open office were filled with what the company describes in a brochure as "The Art Collection of the McDonald's Corporation." In keeping with the overall design of Hamburger Central, these examples of art, scattered throughout the three floors, involve the motif of futurism and space. Ray Kroc's own favorite is a stark departure from the general tone. It is a painting called "A Happy Adventure," specially commissioned from Norman Rockwell in 1971. It hangs in the chairman's own Task Response Module and depicts a group of excited, idealized youngsters crowding around a smiling McDonald's counter-man.

The fully planned "total-concept environment" was intended to create, according to one executive, "an open company that believes in growth, change, dynamics." But open-office planning also offered a number of other advantages. The novel space layout was designed, for instance, to promote the "move factor," calculated at 70 percent. That is, 70 percent of the people would not end up working where they originally started out, yet the renovation cost for each relocation amounted to only twenty-five cents, as compared to ten to twenty dollars a square foot in a conventional office. Further, it was noted that in two years the turnover rate declined from 100 percent, when McDonald's still had its offices downtown, to a level of about 30 percent in Oak Brook. "And people are dressing very colorfully here," observed a very colorfully dressed executive. "They seem to be in a pleasant frame of mind. There's not so much bitchiness anymore."

The bliss that prevails in the open office is to a large extent due to a strange conical-shaped structure on the seventh floor. With a hermetically sealed door, like the hatch of a spacecraft, it stands rooted as Hamburger Central's preeminently solid fixture. A panel on this think tank houses three signal lights: green—PROCEED; yellow—BUZZ; red—STAYOUT.

The think tank was born on the wings of a dilemma. For though achieving the major objectives of the McDonald's space program, not all of its effects had been foreseen. Bitchiness did not at first disappear. In fact, for a while it appeared to be on the increase.

It began with kibitzers leaning over their new TRMs, as suddenly everyone became his burger brother. Examples of rudeness cropped up. There were complaints of fellow workers who trespassed on the undefined space of others. A lot of employees bumped into each other, despite the space; others wandered around aimlessly amid the futuristic art as if they were in a museum. It became clear to designer Pulgram that the "total-concept environment" had to be balanced by a "counter-environment." The space architect consulted with McDonald's president. "There are times when people really need to get away from it all," Pulgram observed.

Fred Turner, after careful consideration, decided on a think tank.

Pulgram knew what Turner meant: "a place for unwinding, contemplation, relaxation, a place to closely relate to other people because there would be no distraction of any kind." The think tank added another $100,000 to the bill.

"The first thing I ever thought of was *Star Trek*," recalls Tom McNulty, the young Jesuit-educated think tank guide from McDonald's public relations firm, Cooper and Golin.

The first whiff of the think tank smells musty. The air conditioner whooshes softly, leaving much of the air to circulate upon itself. Looking earnest, McNulty presses the buzzer. The door shuts and seals with a hush of air, hermetically. Acoustics drain, all sound ebbs away. McNulty's voice sounds distant as he leads the way through a winding corridor, a tunnel of gray, hard-spun, soundproofed fabric.

A vascular organic stillness reigns, inspiring the fear of enclosed places. According to Pulgram, the eerie stillness of the think tank was designed "not to become so quiet as to become spooky." But the spookiness increased at the end of the corridor as McNulty, hushed and solemn as an acolyte, entered a round, enclosed cubicle, much like an egg, lined with the same imitation, narcotic beige suede found throughout Hamburger Central.

The egg-shaped enclosure was the "workroom" adjoining the think tank proper. The workroom is equipped with dim lights, a thick carpet of the same color and material as the walls, a hassock, a beanbag chair, an adjustable desk, and a mysterious box. McNulty opened the lid in the half-light and pulled out a pair of wires tipped with two tiny devices. He explained that the gadget was an alpha pacer, which monitored brain waves by projecting them on a screen. The pacer helped the user choose his "ideal creative state of mind"—an emanation of alpha waves registering on the monitor as tranquil vibrations.

A graphic of a floating hamburger called *Drifting Dimensions* is in the passage leading from the workroom to the actual think tank. Shoes are removed, a second hatch opens. As the visitor enters, footing is lost and he sprawls on the floor of a nine-foot-diameter waterbed—undulating gently as a hidden speaker softly pipes in a melody. The music washes like a fluid, the waterbed rocks gently, the atmosphere takes effect.

The think tank proper offers the shelter of the womb with its soft, pink, fleshy walls. Reversion to infantile, even embryonic, behavior becomes inevitable. The drowse induces a dream.

"All our top people believe in McDonald's," says guide McNulty. "McDonald's is a religion to many of these people." Yet Ray Kroc has apparently never visited the think tank. "It's not something he would jump into," says McNulty.

Kroc looks at young Turner's brainchild from a less complicated vantage. "These young people nowadays have problems," he says, shrugging. "I don't need a think tank. I put two words down on paper and I talk for hours."

The think tank is open to male and female employees, but never at the same time. Mixed, heterosexual thinking is strictly prohibited. But McDonald's executives have not been hesitant to use the tank for its ostensible purpose and several departments have held meetings in it. Advertising and PR people have used it for brainstorming sessions. Any hint of levity about the think sanctum is discouraged by Pulgram, however, who likes to warn, "It's not just a gimmick, a toy. It has to be a very constructive element in the total corporation. Before corporations were on a health-club kick, trying to keep their employees fit. Now corporations live in an age of individuals, and they realize the mind must be healthy, too."

Fred Turner has been one of the more devoted users and

once actually composed a speech in the tank, a very nice speech that was well received by a convention of McDonald's operators.

"Fred Turner spent better than two hours in there, taking notes," recalls Executive V.P. Richard Boylan. "He told me the first hour was very productive, but in the other hour he hit a kind of blank. But, hell, if you can get one good productive hour . . ."

The deepest thinking at Hamburger Central, however, does not take place in the think tank. This occurs in a special room with a door. Here all is discipline, sobriety, and hard-nosed fact. It consists of four-dark-tinted glass walls in the shape of an aquarium, bearing on one side a mammoth, superimposed Arch.

A bust of Ray Kroc is visible inside. Also twelve empty, black-leather chairs, which are filled by the members of the McDonald's board of directors when the highest burger body meets in deliberative session. Most of the enclosure is taken up by a long polished conference table, graced by a centerpiece showing a McDonald's doll in the jaws of an alligator. The base of the figure bears President Fred Turner's personal motto: "When you're up to your ass in alligators, it is easy to forget that your object was to drain the swamp."

On the backs of the twelve chairs are brass-plated names—the members of the board: banker Allen Stults, the money-monitor; David Wallerstein, with theatrical interests; then the financial director, the rotating director, tax specialists, social-science experts, Ray Kroc, Fred Turner; and finally Honorary Director June Martino, the only woman in the masculine world of hamburgers—a dark-haired, iron-willed female who, according to one source, can cook potatoes three hundred different ways.

Known as the "Hamburger Queen," or the "Lucky Lady," June Martino moved to Chicago after high school and took a job as an office clerk for an Italian restauranteur. Not satisfied with the simple secretarial functions, she was soon busy improving the awkward English on the menu and prettifying it with illustrations. In a 1961 series of articles entitled "Women at the Top," the *Chicago American* analyzed the secret of her subsequent rise to success: "Always volunteering for the extra job and never counting the hours of overtime has been the austere but profitable rule in Mrs. Martino's career."

She went to work for Ray Kroc in 1951. Before that she had engaged in a colorful variety of jobs. During a stint as a store detective, her formidable, ramrod, blue-eyed appearance became the bane of shoplifters. She sold bathtubs and helped her husband run an electrical store in Briggsville, Wisconsin. She took a year of accounting at Northwestern University, and in 1943 the Sixth Army Command sent her to school to study electronics, from where she was transferred to "secret war work in industry."

It was her interest in ham radio that introduced the Lucky Lady to her husband, Louis Martino, an electrical engineer who was to make his own contributions to the evolution of Ray Kroc's hamburger venture. In 1959, upon his wife's advice, Louis Martino gave up his electrical engineering business to open a McDonald's stand in Glen Ellyn, Illinois. Five years later, he opened the McDonald's laboratory, in nearby Addison, to streamline further the automation of the hamburger kitchen. Louis Martino created such devices as an electronic computer to measure the moisture content of fish while cooking, as well as computer-run fryers that continuously adjust to the moisture in every potato stick, assuring a uniform degree of brownness.

When Ray Kroc's licensing business began to pick up steam, June Martino was promoted from bookkeeper to secretary-treasurer. Her favorite dish, pasta fagioli (macaroni and beans), shortly took second place to the blander culinary staple her boss was spreading throughout the country; and whenever necessary Mrs. Martino defended the System with the same combative zeal she had brought to each of her other jobs. In 1959 she fired off an angry letter to *Fortune* magazine in response to an article decrying the defacement of the American highway by such signs as McDonald's "rainbow arch." "Uninterrupted scenery, too, can get pretty monotonous," she wrote, describing the McDonald's trademark as "only a way of humanizing what is still an overwhelming landscape."

June Martino (now an honorary director) became the Lucky Lady because in the early start-up days of McDonald's she took her salary in stock instead of cash. It made her rich.

"Seventy million dollars," Chairman Kroc mused in retrospect. "You know, I must have thought a lot of her. But June obtained her wealth. She was entitled to every penny of it. She worked and sweated and did everything under the sun, and then she got out of it. And when I saw that she had gone out, I said, 'Well, you might as well go out on me. Get out. Make room for someone else. The business is for the needy, not the greedy.'"

Hamburger Central stands as the realization of Ray Kroc's merchandizing dream. His model, through the years of slow, painstaking formulization, had been equally ambitious—none other than the world's biggest merchandizer, founded by fellow Chicagoan Richard Warren Sears and Alvah Curtis Roebuck in 1887. Whenever Kroc was having problems at McDonald's he would envy the organization and delegation of authority that was shown by Sears, Roebuck, which he did not even consider in the same class as general department stores. "It's a brand and a breed of loyalty of some kind," Kroc believes, "an esprit de corps, whatever it is, that's inbred in Sears, Roebuck people and that others don't have."

As a young man, Ray Kroc had read much about the exploits of Richard Warren Sears. It was said of Sears, the son of a small-town midwestern farmer, that he could sell a "breath of air." His retail empire eventually became an American institution, frequented even by presidents. Calvin Coolidge was a loyal Sears, Roebuck customer, and later Franklin D. Roosevelt, who would suggest that the best way to teach the Kremlin a lesson in American superiority was to bomb it with a Sears, Roebuck catalog.

Kroc was equally impressed with the catalog, a book he credits with having influenced his entire life and philosophy. It taught him the secrets of distribution and of appealing to the mass market. He took from it the virtues of organization and thrift, and when he set out to mass-retail hamburgers, fries, malts, pies, cookies, and soft drinks, he applied the same methods with which Sears had transformed the sales of jewelry, furniture, dishes, wagons, harnesses, saddles, buggies, and musical instruments. Their mass-retailing techniques were already changing distribution patterns when the American-style hamburger was born at the 1904 Saint Louis World's Fair.* Fittingly, it was created by a harried cook who slapped a broiled patty on a bun to serve the throngs at the fairgrounds. The hamburger was simple to prepare. It could be served fast and proved ideally suited to the sped-up tempo of American life. Nineteenth-century accounts of U.S. habits and customs had already noted that hordes of Americans wolfed their food on the run, bolting sandwiches and coffee in station restaurants while trains stood panting outside.

The Saint Louis exposition also introduced two other remarkably simple food products, iced tea and the ice-cream cone. And these products would venture from the Midwest as harbingers of a native way of eating based increasingly on speed and convenience. The automobile played a crucial role in this. The year before the Saint Louis fair, Henry Ford had sold his first horseless carriage, and in its wake sprang up a whole new category of restaurant staples comprising the limited, quick-service menu of fast food.

Like Sears, Kroc made speed part and parcel of the mer-

* The birthplace of the American hamburger is also claimed by New Haven, Connecticut, where the first ground-beef patty on a bun was supposedly served in 1900 by a small diner called Louis Lunch. In early 1974 *Nation's Restaurant News* reported that Louis Lunch might be bulldozed.

chandising package. Sears had put to work the first automatic
mail-opener capable of slitting open 27,000 orders an hour.
Young girls processed the mail by shooting the orders through
a pneumatic tube into stockrooms where mountains of merchandise moved endlessly by conveyor belts and gravity
chutes to staggered assembly points. The operation was
broken down into twenty-seven steps, enabling Sears to fill
and ship an order in the amazingly short span of one day—a
system so efficient that Henry Ford studied it before launching
his automobile assembly line in Detroit.

Ray Kroc showed much the same flair for utilizing the benefits of technology and efficiency planning. On the modern
McDonald's grills, winking lights tell countermen when to flip
over the hamburger. The cooking capacity per fryer was constantly improved until it reached $230 worth of french fries
per hour. Louis Martino's research lab and a small group of
equipment makers furnished McDonald's with a stream of
such continually updated gadgets designed to automate the
serving and cooking of food to the ultimate degree: premeasured scoops, ketchup and mustard dispensers, computer-
run fryers, infrared warning lights, instruments for testing the
solidity of raw potatoes and the fluffiness of shakes. Nothing—
as Hamburger Central proudly boasts—was left to chance.
McDonald's even recently established a grandly named Department of Technology that has begun test runs on electronic
cash registers and "direct-draw shake machines," that would
enable an employee to simultaneously draw four different-
flavored shakes from the device.

What such rigid standardization could do for the profit picture was demonstrated by the frail, lackluster french fry. Once
a haphazardly cooked snack with a low profit yield, it turned
into a substantial money-maker, with approximately 40 percent sales increase each year. The systematic approach taught
to all managers and franchisees eliminated even a few crumbs
of waste. For a corporation buying trainloads of potatoes
annually, a few extra french fries dropped carelessly into each

bag could have a serious effect on annual earnings. But using Hamburger Central's famed wide-mouthed scoop, an unskilled teen-age employee could funnel and stack bags of fries identical in content. In a way the premeasured scoop was symbolic of the whole merchandizing scheme. It not only avoided costly spillage but actually gave an impression of abundance by making each bag appear to be slightly overfilled.

The same safeguards were built into the prepacked, prefrozen, premeasured ground-beef-and-fat patty. In 1968, after years of testing, the basic 1.6-ounce automated hamburger was quickly overshadowed by an even more successful model: two meat patties divided by a middle bun, complete with onion flakes, slivers of pickle, and a smidgen of cheese. Big Mac!

An even more awesome hunk of meat, the Quarter Pounder, followed and proved so profitable that between 1971 and 1972 Hamburger Central's profits jumped $10 million.

Years of development and testing preceded each new product that came on the market. In 1971 McDonald's began experiments with an ice-cream cone that appeared a year later as Triple Ripple. A drawn-out process of test-marketing in various parts of the country finally resulted in the national distribution of Egg McMuffin, a breakfast item of toasted muffin with melted cheese, fried egg, and Canadian bacon that allowed McDonald's to open early. The Egg McMuffin was christened by Fred Turner's wife, Patty.

The Sears approach to handling orders was complemented in Ray Kroc's hamburger stands. Each McDonald's functioned as a sophisticated center for production, quality control, retail sales, marketing, and consumption. In effect, a McFactory that followed the Sears, Roebuck volume formula, with low profits on each item and large *aggregate* profits from total sales.

Like all the major fast-food staples—pizza, fried chicken, doughnuts, and hot dogs—hamburgers offered little that was new. In 1925, when Howard Johnson opened his first roadside eateries, the public favored practically the same items popular today. However, the new marketing techniques homogenized American eating habits.

By the time Ray Kroc discovered the franchise, it had already proved an effective marketing device. Franchising allowed rapid growth because most of the capital for expansion was put up by the franchisee; and during the fifties, when it flourished, franchising took fast food to wherever the consumers were. In the post–World War II era that meant the burgeoning suburbs. The roadside and the suburb were closely connected, so when Ray Kroc began selling McDonald's franchises in 1955 he bypassed the cities and drove out to the new developments.

He had not been alone on the road. Nor were franchises confined merely to fast food. Within a few years the landscape was seeded with familiar trademark names, including service franchises such as Martinizing Dry Cleaner and United Rent-All, hotels and motels like Holiday Inn and Marriott, and product distribution outlets like Aamco Transmission Centers. But the greatest impact was made by the promoters of fast food who sold licenses for everything, from "Glori-Fried" chicken to tacos, Duch hamburgers, pancakes, and wienerschnitzel. The early fast-food franchises became legendary success stories—Dunkin Donuts, Dairy Queen, Kentucky Fried Chicken, McDonald's—and drew a host of imitators who applied the same formula of mass-menu standardization and quick service.

The refinements of uniformity in product had been pioneered by Henry Ford, who allowed his Model T customers to choose any color they liked—as long as it was black. Similar consistency and sameness became the hallmark of Ray Kroc's assembly-line hamburger. McDonald's could not be the place for the rugged individualist who wanted his hamburger grilled and garnished according to taste. "The minute you get into customizing you're on an individual basis," Chairman Kroc said. "The cost of the product is exactly the same, but the *labor* triples." So the founder would get irritated if a patron ordered his raw onion put under the broiler.

"We can't do that," Ray Kroc would lament.

At Hamburger Central in Oak Brook resides the control that makes the thousands of McDonald's stands tick in "uncustomized" harmony, turning out consistency and sameness in product and service from coast to coast. Every facet comes under its wing—from purchasing, supply, and marketing to law, finance, real estate. Central sells hamburgers in Hiroshima, Hong Kong, Omaha, and Munich. Its three floors of specialized executives are attuned to every winking grill and sputtering french fry in kitchens from Paris to Pocatello; from the Florida Keys to the Great Australian Barrier Reef; from the Ginza to Broadway and Watts. They are fluent about zoning laws, management, competition, labor unrest, union activities, research labs, city hall, state legislatures, Capitol Hill, the White House.

The franchisee buying a McDonald's license soon discovers that the ideal of the American Dream is in reality submission to the dictums of Hamburger Central. But by bowing to a worklife regimented by Ray Kroc and his subordinates, he is given the security of a System that has been proven to make money. The System, it is stressed, will continue to make him money as long as he abides by the rules, and for nearly $200,000—about half of it in cash—Hamburger Central sells him a twenty-year license. Then it picks his site, buys the land, builds the store, fills it with equipment, and rents it to him for a stiff 8.5 percent of gross annual revenues, plus a 3 percent annual franchise fee. The System works especially well for McDonald's. "We're just like the Mafia," *Time* magazine quoted one of Hamburger Central's financial officers, "we skim it right off the top."

Basically what the franchisee buys from Hamburger Central, though, is something less tangible than the System. He buys the demonstrated profitability of a name, a symbol to identify his goods and distinguish them from his competitors'. The name is the key to his success. The registered trademark is Hamburger Central's primary stock, its most valuable possession. Early in his career the founder realized that a hamburger chain called "Kroc's" was out of the question. "McDonald's" harked back soothingly to a nursery rhyme and an eccentric old farmer who conversed with animals. The name possessed instant recognition. It appealed to the six-year-old mind, just as the bland food appealed to the six-year-old palate and, as a later Hamburger Central study would confirm, in three out of four families it is the children who decide where to eat.

The trademark gave birth to the System. It was the single seed that pushed forth Big Mac, Hamburger Central, Hamburger University, hamburger workers, suppliers, land, leaseholds, hamburger millionaires. The growing family of trademarks that moved into the franchisee's stand even took precedence over McDonald's vaunted equipment and central management control.

Strict corporate supervision regulated the licencees' use of these. Cellophane, escalator, and aspirin were just a few brand names that had been lost simply through lack of vigilance. Others like Xerox and 3M Company were fighting to prevent cancellation of their trademarks, Xerox and Scotch Tape. And Johnson and Johnson was battling against misuse of its Band-Aid trademark. Hamburger Central urged its far-flung personnel to report all infringements, promising the kind of quick legal action it sprang on United Airlines for the jocular use of "Big Mac" in a promotional flight brochure. In its own internal publications, Hamburger Central stressed its determination "to police all uses of our trademarks."

A corps of roving "field supervisors" even drops in a couple of times a month (usually unexpectedly) on each franchised and company-run store. A policing force, they maintain order throughout the empire, working out of eight district, eight regional, and nineteen subregional offices. The network included offices in forty American cities as of the end of 1974, each of which is fully staffed with managers providing expertise and directives on advertising, promotion, real estate, remodeling, training, and restaurant operations.

Hamburger Central's accounting department holds seminars for all McDonald's accountants. Its legal department sends out bulletins on the lighting of the American flag. Four times a year owners and managers in each marketing area attend Central–directed training sessions. Management is also schooled at hallowed Hamburger University, which also offers refresher courses and postgrad seminars in Hamburgerology, and Central even supplies brochures to teach operators how to communicate with college students. "Talk to the students in a direct manner, they call it 'talking straight.' . . . They would say 'tell it like it is.' "

The corporate bible is a 385-page operations manual, a Gideon of the Golden Arches crammed with details down to the minutiae of running the hamburger business. Besides the all-encompassing manual, managers receive regular editions of *Management News,* while another internal publication, *Crew's Views,* is directed at the young workers. Licencees, however, are reserved an exclusive monthly issue of *Insight,* a top echelon bulletin emanating from McDonald's Public Affairs Office. *Insight* reports union activities and other signs of restiveness within McDonald's labor force. It contains news of product and equipment innovations, promotional schemes, and future plans, but its chief function is as an organ of business related intelligence—from inside hints on how to pay less income tax to a monthly competitive analysis column. The latter has featured such things as reports that Colonel Sanders of Kentucky Fried Chicken was seeking a visa to visit the People's Republic of China and that KFC was planning to purchase Chinese chickens for its new Hong Kong outlet.

This control exercised by Hamburger Central has proved a sturdy bulwark against such economic ills as rising labor costs, inflation, and consumerism. During the first half of 1973, when meat prices registered record highs, Central reported a 43 percent jump in income and construction of 151 new units or about one a day. For 1974 Fred Turner announced a record opening of 420 new stores. Little wonder that Hamburger Central could boast that McDonald's was "recession-proof," and as the national economy went deeper into an inflationary tailspin, events appeared to bear out this assertion.

For instance, when it came to the question of possible price ceilings on food items, a fiscal policy that Central openly abhors, McDonald's received support from economists and politicians, while Secretary of Agriculture Earl Butz supported price increases that allowed McDonald's to keep prices rising. A former director of Ralston-Purina, which also owns the Jack in the Box hamburger chain, Butz chided that "only damn fools" would favor price controls on food. Even when President Nixon chimed in with a suggestion that Americans eat fish rather than meat, Hamburger Central was not worried, since McDonald's happened to be the country's biggest retailer of fish, surpassing all other companies in 1971 by selling over 19 million pounds!

McDonald's approach to the purchase and distribution of such massive amounts of foodstuffs and related products has given it a special niche in the food-service industry. Its outlets consume forests of paper supplies, mountains of ground beef, miles of french fries, rivers of Coca-Cola and coffee. Since antitrust legislation prohibits the franchisor from being a supplier for its franchised units, the McDonald's headquarters sells no products. If it did, it would be guilty of a "tie-in," in which a company both specifies what its customer must purchase and is at the same time the supplier.

McDonald's franchises spend well over a half billion dollars annually on a vast array of supplies, ranging from burgers, buns, pickles, and napkins to trash receptacles, cleaning solvents, and the spray guns handled by busboys to kill dirt on tables. All of this money is funneled into "approved" company suppliers, whose dizzying rise in annual earnings has steadily followed the pattern of McDonald's. No contracts exist with the dozen or so major suppliers. For the record, McDonald's System is a *service* company limited to delivering a *service* rather than producing and selling its own food or restaurant equipment.

But Hamburger Central specifies what the licensee must purchase *and* from whom to buy it, the object being to guarantee the uniformity of standards so crucial to the entire system. Thus it became the rule that the suppliers who began with McDonald's have stayed with McDonald's.

"They started with the first store," the chairman explained in an interview. "They are still our prime suppliers. We never leave a supplier. He's got to be a dirty bastard. He's got to try to cheat. He's got to do something bad before we lose him. Our suppliers grow with us."

4

KISS

"Keep It Simple, Stupid"

In 1968, Hamburger Central ushered in a new period, the post–Kroc era, which saw the chairman take his first gingerly step to the side as he appointed thirty-five-year-old Fred Turner president of the company. Subsequent years saw the rapid disappearance of the founder's fondest principles—they would witness the end of the Formula and the most serious violation of Kroc's favorite business motto, this one borrowed from his old friend Colonel Sanders: KISS—"Keep It Simple, Stupid."

Under Turner, the garish, mightily illumined drive-ins Kroc had made famous disappeared; the red-and-white-tile exteriors were replaced by dull-brown brick, lots of plate glass, and a sleek-sloping, double-mansard, shingled roof. The pulsing, exuberant Golden Arches were streamlined into the current subdued, nonbiodegradable yellow plastic logo that rears more gently from the road. But the most noticeable change took place inside the stands, which were now called "restaurants," boasting plastic seats and tables and an interior modeled in a consistent pattern of "escape" motifs.

"We're trying to dispel the old feeling that McDonald's is a noisy, gaudy, neon-lighted hamburger stand," said one company executive. McDonald's "escape" atmosphere followed a general trend, as did the increasing asexuality of the restaurant interiors, most commonly decorated with the neuter characters from McDonaldland—Big Mac, Ronald McDonald, Captain Crook, the Hamburglar, Mayor McCheese, and Evil Grimace. On the adult level, the interiors began to concentrate on "themes"—a nautical theme in Boston, a campus theme near the University of California in Los Angeles, a chalet-type in Michigan, the replica of an artist's sky-lighted studio in New York's Greenwich Village, and a Western flavor in Dallas, with arches branded on hitching posts. In some places McDonald's even appropriated the airs of *haute cuisine*. In Maryland and Los Angeles hostesses wearing long gowns served Big Macs and Quarter Pounders at candlelight dinners, and in Atlanta shakes were served in crystal goblets. The company had hired a new ad agency that played down the prosaic business of eating a cheap mushy hamburger. The "McDonald's experience" was to be stressed instead.

Hamburger Central's ambitious expansion and conversion program pointed up its main area of interest. "McDonald's knows real estate like the back of its thick patties," the financial journal *Barron's* noted in April, 1971, when the company already carried land, buildings, and leaseholds to the tune of well over $100 million. Examining McDonald's revenue dollar a year later, America's leading fast-food-service magazine supported Wall Street's opinion that McDonald's was not so much a hamburger empire as a gigantic real estate concern.

In 1973, real estate, franchise rentals and company-owned stores, for the first time provided more than half of Hamburger Central's income. Thus, under conditions of an inflationary rate higher than the national average (McDonald's prices have doubled in the past decade), real estate has been the bulwark allowing Central planners to adapt to new economic demands. And Kroc's "baby," that once nestled close to church steeples and carports, was also fleeing suburbia. It had found a haven of real estate and mighty profits amid crime, smog, and congestion under the bright lights downtown, in the urban core, in the neighborhoods of the workers and the poor, in upper class residential areas, and down in the ghetto.

The move into the heart of American cities had come as a deliberate and necessary step to broaden McDonald's market. The decision was made by full-dress sessions of the highest burger body in Oak Brook. It was a decision that implied far-reaching consequences for the future course of the company. Ray Kroc had always shunned the big city and had guided McDonald's to prosperity by following the automobile, but there had come an end to the endless road, and after phenomenal growth during nearly two decades, the close of the sixties saw the U.S. fast-food market approaching a state of glut. Only two areas were left for continued expansion and these were the cities at home and the developed, industrialized countries abroad, primarily European countries and Japan, where the American-style mass-menu meal was rapidly gaining ground.

McDonald's expansion overseas proceeded with relative ease, compared to the problems it encountered in its strange new urban environment. Suddenly Oak Brook's small-town hierarchy was beset by big-city headaches. Protests and demonstrations followed the planting of the arches, and wherever it went in the city, McDonald's seemed to stumble on a hornet's nest of outraged citizens. Out in suburbia it had been able to sprawl contentedly, but in the city McDonald's was attacked by people from virtually every socioeconomic and racial stratum. Merchants denounced McDonald's for driving them to the wall financially and jacking up real estate prices. Ethnic neighborhoods protested that McDonald's destroyed the character of the community. Ghetto residents objected to white hamburger domination and substandard food.

Teen-age workers complained that they received the lowest
wages in the country. Even the genteel demonstrated with
placards and petitions, horrified by the idea of a hamburger
stand in their neighborhood. In Chicago, Cleveland, San
Francisco, and New York, civic groups of all stripes found a
common butt of enmity. In the summer of 1974 one anti-
McDonald's leader in New York went so far as to predict that
the whole country might learn to hate McDonald's "just on
principle."

Ironically, it was McDonald's high visibility that served as a
touchstone for the passions its presence set loose. This local
prominence throughout the country had been achieved as the
result of one of the costliest and most thoroughgoing PR and
ad campaigns in American corporate history. A massive
apparatus of patty propaganda had made the trademark a
household word, placing the McDonald's hamburger—the "all-
American meal"—next to the flag, Mom, and apple pie. An
unremitting campaign identifying McDonald's with every
form of patriotism, community concern, and loudly-trumpeted
benefactions had dinned the name into public consciousness.
This campaign had been so successful that on the occasion of
his seventieth birthday, Ray Kroc could happily announce, "I
have had the satisfaction of seeing McDonald's become an
American tradition. Such a dream could only be realized in
America."

The chairman made this pleasing observation at a time
when McDonald's visibility had already turned into its most
conspicuous liability. For a lot of understandable and as many
inexplicable reasons, McDonald's just made a lot of people
mad. The deeper roots of this antipathy, though, were to be
found in the changed political and economic climate, rampant
inflation, and an aroused consumer public. The first large-scale
resistance to the Golden Arches at the start of the seventies
coincided with a general mood of national discontent. Mc-
Donald's self-appointed status as an "American tradition" had
come at a time when all American traditions had suddenly

become suspect. It was a time for questioning the host of shibboleths that paraded in all-American garb, which in Mc-Donald's case constituted a spar-spangled wardrobe. It had an All-American Marching Band, and an All-American Team. Its All-American Meal was to be served by specifically pre-scribed All-American Boys. American of the Year, Ray Kroc, was largely responsible for the insistence that the hamburger stands fly the flag around the clock and he identified his boast-ful billion-burger signs as an unofficial index of the country's health. America led the world in hamburgers sold, and what was good for McDonald's was good for the country.

McDonald's was far from being the only example of corpo-rate cant in American life but, because of its prominence, it served as a convenient target for the residents of ghettos and low-income communities. Inner-city people seemed to vent their frustration on McDonald's for the same reasons that demonstrators in exploited countries singled out the U.S. em-bassy or the offices of Yankee corporations, for by purveying poor food, high promises, and minimum wages, McDonald's became a similar symbol of the system. In many communities the brightly lit McFactory was seen as the neighborhood col-onizer, taking out huge profits without giving anything in return.

Before launching its full-scale urban offensive, Hamburger Central had run into sporadic resistance in suburbs and small towns. Generally the objections had centered on aesthetic grounds as communities took exception to the eye-popping arches and storefronts. In a few cases, different zoning and architectural review boards had been able to force McDonald's to lower its prominent profile, but in the end they had usually been powerless to halt Big Mac's advance. Residents of Cam-bridge, Massachusetts, for instance, protested in vain when one of the city's only two pre–Civil War Greek Revival land-mark buildings was torn down. In San Francisco, massive opposition by unions, the mayor, and community groups man-aged to stall the chain for as long as a year before caving in to unrelenting pressure. In almost every case, the full panoply of McDonald's resources, legal and otherwise, was able to overcome all resistance.

It was New York that presented Hamburger Central with the most sustained opposition in its twenty-year history. McDonald's made up for its belated entry into this area with a blitz that in less than two years spread outlets from the Lower West Side in Greenwich Village to the Upper West Side, around Carnegie Hall, into Harlem and the boroughs. Its chief area of operations was in what soon came to be known as the "burg of Manhattan." All of McDonald's resources of money, propaganda, and real estate expertise were thrown behind the invasion. Mayor Abraham Beame's campaign consultant was engaged as a public relations adviser and, with money apparently no object, the stands arose in short order on the choicest sites.

By the summer of 1974 Manhattan hosted twenty-two McDonald's stands and New Yorkers had been presented with a *fait accompli*—all the while McDonald's was building, Hamburger Central had maintained a strict policy of keeping any identifying signs from the construction sites.

Big Mac had entered the city behind a Trojan horse of high unmarked sidewalk fences—the Big Apple had been bored from within. The outcry of New Yorkers was resounding, in some cases hysterical. The issue flared to emotional heights as an anti-McDonald's campaign got under way that enlisted the aid of a congressman and prominent civic leaders; an anti-McDonald's petition with 11,000 signatures was delivered to the mayor's office; people threatened to throw themselves in front of McDonald's bulldozers and *New York* magazine came out with a cover showing a Godzilla-like hamburger eating the city. Communities all over Manhattan made it clear they didn't want Big Mac as a neighbor.

In dealing with protest, Hamburger Central seemed to hold to a domino theory—if one stand fell, the whole chain might crumble. This appeared to be its policy in the inner cities and its diplomatic accommodation in the suburbs. By bowing to the demands of neighborhood self-determination, it was believed, not only Big Mac's prestige would suffer but its whole economic future would be jeopardized. Thus not even the most stubborn opposition had been able to stay the burger people, except in one New York locale, where Hamburger Central for the first time chose not to exercise its self-proclaimed right to build outlets anywhere zoning and city laws allowed.

The field of Central's defeat was hardly typical of neighborhoods in cities across America where attempts had failed to keep McDonald's out. This was an aristocratic Manhattan enclave, and the conflict that sprang up in the summer of 1974 became known as the "Battle of Lexington," after the site of hostilities—the corner of Sixty-sixth Street and Lexington Avenue, where McDonald's had razed a funeral parlor to erect a subdued town house hamburger parlor, which it promised would be very "tasteful" and blend in well with the area. But the community it had chosen was not just a "good neighborhood," *The Wall Street Journal* pointed out, but the "best neighborhood"—the home of New York's power structure, including the chairman of the world's most influential bank, David Rockefeller of the Chase Manhattan; the prestigious investment bankers Lehman and Loeb; Vietnam war architect and former LBJ confidant McGeorge Bundy; Establishment figures like Mrs. Whitney North Seymour; media bigwigs, editors, and influential writers, like Theodore White, who wrote Ray Kroc a personal letter that concluded on a quietly threatening note, "The enmity of this community is not a matter to invite lightly." Hamburger Central agreed and quietly abandoned the site.

The outcome of the Battle of Lexington did not dampen McDonald's expansionary zeal, however. The newly built McDonald's across from Madison Square Garden showed the reason why Hamburger Central was prepared to fight for every inch of urban ground, as the stand set a new monthly record by selling $190,000 worth of fast food. Euphorically, it drew up blueprints for a twenty-four-hour walk-up store inside a Manhattan office building, following Kentucky Fried Chicken, which was also planning to set up its first twenty-four-hour store in Times Square.

"When you're green you're growing," went one of Chairman Kroc's favorite mottoes; "when you're ripe you rot." To the founder, McDonald's was still in a green stage, having hardly tapped the full profit potential. After blitzing the inner cities, Kroc confidently predicted further invasions of hitherto untouched territories. He talked about setting up shop inside plants and factories and sports stadiums. Howard Johnson was already catering some school food programs, and one McDonald's outlet already did a roaring business on the University of Cincinnati campus. In 1971 mall units and a smaller version of the basic design known as the "Mini-Mac" were introduced and a new thirty-variable real estate selection computer program was installed at the corporate headquarters to plot new territorial objectives. More real estate was added as Central began to concentrate on the development of McDonaldland, a children's playground stocked with garish characters like Mayor McCheese, the Hamburglar, Captain Crook, Evil Grimace, and Ronald McDonald. A number of these were built in Chicago and California and more are on the way. One, planned for Las Vegas, is to rival Disneyland in size and sophistication.

Hamburger espionage by competitors remains a constant source of anxiety on every level of administration, and McDonald's execs are told that the walls have ears. Despite the open office, the world of McDonald's is closed. Consequently a general feeling of suspicion dogged the authors during a visit to Hamburger Central, who were told that other chains were irredeemably bent on filching promotional schemes and plans for new site locations. Taco Bell, a West Coast taco chain, was reputed to be locating, whenever possible, near a McDonald's

stand and that another rival allegedly paid an anonymous visit
to the facilities of its Philadelphia supplier.

But nothing was as irksome as Burger King opening an
outlet across the street from the Oak Brook McDonald's, Ray
Kroc's pet stand. "I'll see those sons of bitches in hell," he
fumed.

The actions of rivals have left the founder with a rich fund
for scorn and rancor. He was particularly exercised when
Burger Chef, McDonald's number three competitor, took his
own QSC (Quality Service Cleanliness) formula and added
another C—for "Courtesy"—in its "Four Pillars of the Burger
Chef Way." Kroc in an interview assailed his competitor with
an adapted Kipling quote:

> They may copy my style,
> And they may imitate me.
> But they can't read my mind,
> And I'll leave them a mile and a half behind.

As a result of the secrecy enjoined upon employees, managers, and executives, McDonald's does not mix with the rest
of the fast-food industry. Ray Kroc spurns being identified
with any of them. Just as he thinks of Sears, Roebuck in a
category separate from mere department stores, he does not
consider McDonald's to be in the same common league of fast-
food chains.

"I don't know people that are in the industry," Kroc told the
authors. "I know my own people. I don't want our people to go
into seminars with the industry. I expect nothing from the
industry and I intend to give them nothing. This is a business
where you guard zealously your so-called trade secrets."

Ray Kroc became more accessible as he withdrew from the
daily operation of the company. At seventy-two, he is still
spry, a dapper dresser in a way typical of successful salesmen,
with bold matching colors, very shiny shoes, and everything
on his person neatly in place. He is of small build, grown

plump over the years. His features are pink and uncompli-cated, but the jaw thrusts aggressively, the blue eyes pierce. When he is in good spirits he glows and his smile turns mis-chievous. As chairman of the board and McDonald's majority owner with 20 percent of the stock, he is one of the country's wealthiest men. In 1973, McDonald's stock reached $70 and his 7 million shares swelled his fortune to $500 million, putting him in the ranks of the dozen richest tycoons.

When his first McDonald's opened in 1955, he had set out, by his own account, to take the "joint" out of the hamburger and the "b.s." out of "business." It was his drive and stamina that stretched the company further each year. Attesting to this is the golden statuette in Ray Kroc's Task Response Module at Hamburger Central. Resembling a Hollywood Oscar, it is inscribed "Ray Kroc, the All-Time Mr. McDonald's."

The chairman's TRM is the largest open office in the head-quarters building, but its function is mostly ceremonial. The company is run by Fred Turner. Kroc does not bother with the financial end of it at all. "I am interested in the brick and mortar and the equipment and the retail service," he says proudly, seeing his role today more like that of a coach: "The agitator," he enthuses, "the motivator, the never-satisfied-type of guy." In this capacity he roams the open road in a chauffeured limousine, leaving his TRM, the think tank, and Hamburger Central far behind, to visit McDonald's stands out along the highways he used to travel as a salesman. He likes to pull in unannounced, scanning the parking lot for cigarette butts and papers. Inside he straightens napkin dispensers, opens a trash bin, and samples hamburgers in the kitchen. He is especially fussy about toilets. They have to sparkle.

When he is not traveling by limousine, the founder has other means of transportation at his disposal—his Grumman jet, which seats seventeen and can fly anywhere in the world; his seventy-two-foot yacht in Florida; an antique Model A; a fire-engine-red Cadillac; and even a private railroad car, the

"McDonald's Special," sporting Golden Arches embossed in the form of a crown, which Harry Truman once rode between Saint Louis and Independence, Missouri. Ray Kroc is also the proud possessor of twenty converted Greyhound buses, which he leases to the company for a dollar a year. Each is equipped with plush swivel chairs, a radio, telephone, stereo, color TV, an elaborate galley, shower, and washrooms, and each of the buses bears the name Big Mac in the destination window. Cost: $150,000 apiece. Use: public relations, field trips for orphans, and public-service outings.

Kroc's home base is a 6,000-square-foot apartment located in a section of Chicago's Lakeshore Drive known as the Gold Coast. His Florida winter home is in Fort Lauderdale's ultra-posh Bay Colony section. There his residence consists of a sprawling, cotton-white villa. His backyard is a natural channel. In addition, Kroc has his own replica of the nursery-rhyme farm celebrated as "Old McDonald's"—a 210-acre ranch in California's Santa Ynez Valley near the Danish-style tourist town of Solvang, famed for its pastries and pristine cleanliness. The ranch displays the brand of the double arches and has been stocked with forty cows of all shapes and hues, a huge black bull, Arabian horses, and golden retrievers. There are test kitchens and breeding paraphernalia, and cooks cater the occasional hamburger seminars conducted on the ranch, which allow McDonald's executives to mix business with horseback riding, swimming, and loud, festive barbecues. The twenty-room ranchhouse is also the home of the Kroc Foundation, dedicated to the conquest of arthritis, diabetes, and multiple sclerosis, and headed by Dr. Robert L. Kroc, the chairman's brother. Kroc's neighbor is another famous rancher, movie star Jimmy Stewart.

The founder keeps active. He is said to dabble in a few stocks, some with names like Spacelabs and American Pet Motels, an outfit that provides luxurious lodging for high-rolling dogs and cats. He is also building a Hamburger Museum at his ranch.

One thing the founder no longer does is introduce new menu extensions or start new business ventures. His invention of the Hula Burger—a slice of pineapple between two buns—was a disaster. A roast beef sandwich shared a similar fate. Failure also dogged Kroc's elegant outlets for a genteel and aristocratic hamburger. Two "Ramond's" were actually opened in Beverly Hills and Chicago, and soon closed. A similar miscalculation caused the untimely end of the Jane Dobbins Pie Shop, which Kroc opened in Pasadena.

But Ray Kroc, like all inveterate salesmen, cannot live without all-consuming commitment to something new. Recently he found his passion in the San Diego Padres, the National League baseball team that earned notice as the "losingest" club in the major leagues.

In his shrinelike office at McDonald's Oak Brook headquarters, the chairman is surrounded by mementos and framed inspirational messages, including passages from Democritus, Plutarch, and the Declaration of Independence. Among the busts of Lincoln, Ronald McDonald, and a milk cow is a Distinguished Citizens Award from the Cook County Department of Corrections, also a glass-enclosed check from the brokerage firm of Paine, Webber in the amount of $17,572,500. There are yacht trophies, a huge blow-up of his Model A car, an electronic clock showing hamburger time around the world, a porcelain statue of triple-bun hero Big Mac. Somehow they are the trappings of a bygone era, a simpler time when there was no Hamburger Central or Hamburger University, when a burger was still a burger and not the "McDonald's experience."

The old days were better. The sudden spate of crises that has deluged McDonald's as the company entered its third decade of existence must have been bewildering to Kroc. Consumer criticism was one such crisis. One New York restaurant critic concluded that McDonald's food was "irredeemably horrible, with no saving graces whatever." Neither was it that cheap.

Big Mac, the doyen of Hamburger Central's mass menu, at eighty-five cents worked out to between $4 and $4.20 per pound of ground beef.

In its new urban setting, McDonald's was also fast losing another of its proud assets. In 1955 he had made it his goal to change the hamburger joint image and make it a haven of good, clean family fun. But eighteen years later the original image had returned, stronger than ever, as Hamburger Central continued its penetration of crime-ridden areas, goaded by the need to locate where profits were highest. "Instead of a symbol of good old family entertainment," one anti-McDonald's vigilante charged, the stands were "becoming synonymous with fear, loitering, drugs, trash, and congestion." A massive demonstration in San Francisco's Mission District against the construction of a McDonald's outlet in the community cited "hamburger joints" as favorite hangouts for junkies, drug dealers, bikers, and pill-pushers. Similar fears led to protests by residents around Manhattan's Third Avenue and Eighty-fourth Street, an area with five Methadone clinics and 2,500 addict transients.

By the time Ray Kroc surrendered active control, families had already become an extinct species at some of his inner-city stands. In Chicago's tough West Side ghetto, a number of McDonald's operators kept shotguns near the grill, while, in New York and San Francisco, stands were policed by guards dressed as managers and muscular "customers" with handcuffs tied to their belts. Even the chairman's vaunted C for Cleanliness fell victim to the changed times when Washington, D.C. health inspectors briefly closed down one outlet. (It has since reopened.)

The burgeoning growth of post–World War II families had set off the McDonald's chain reaction and explosion of profits. He had harnessed the families to light up his arches from coast to coast, but the time of burgeoning families was over and his model family with "one car going on two" belonged to the fifties. The poor were increasingly the segment of the population that ate McDonald's food.

The end of the sixties had also seen the tarnishing of the franchise—the method of marketing formerly embraced as the answer to every American who dreamed of becoming a small businessman in the age of giant corporations. Franchising had been hailed in business magazines, at expositions, at franchise shows, and in the popular press. *Newsweek* called it "the daffiest boom of the decade." It was a game, the magazine rhapsodized, "that everyone can play—from the biggest names in show business and the craftiest financiers of Wall Street to the man in the street." But by 1970 the boom had collapsed under the weight of declining profits and oversaturation.

From the outset, franchisees had earned a reputation for being the least sophisticated among the investing public. Gullible and mesmerized by the idea of becoming small capitalists, thousands lost their life savings in shady ventures that promised to follow real success stories like McDonald's and Kentucky Fried Chicken. While revelations of franchise fraud and profiteering by other firms forced congressional investigations, Hamburger Central was gradually losing its character as a franchise company. The franchise was becoming less and less important in the further expansion of McDonald's. By buying back more licenses each year from owner-operators, Hamburger Central was rapidly increasing the number of far more profitable company-run stands. By 1973 30 percent of the McDonald's outlets were operated from Oak Brook directly.

In the grim new decade of the seventies, even Ray Kroc's workhorse of fast-food success, the automobile, appeared to fall victim to America's suddenly crimping life-style as a national speed limit was imposed for the first time. To soothe stockholders a report that Hamburger Central did not expect a "sales volume decrease because of the gasoline shortage" was released. McDonald's standing on the New York Stock Exchange continued to plummet, sliding down from an all-time high of seventy dollars a share, to a low of twenty-five dollars by the fall of 1974. The opening of a record 420 outlets was seen by some security analysts as reckless overexpansion and they continued to advise their clients to stay away from McDonald's. At Hamburger Central the market crisis exceeded all others. (The stock eventually recovered but remains approximately 30 points below its peak value.)

During the sixties conditions had been very similar to the waves of speculation that had sent stocks zooming in the twenties. For a few this was a time to clean up. On the exchange floor and at the brokerage houses, in the banks and in the boardrooms, gigantic transactions took place. Paper shuffled, moving mountains of money and the McDonald's stock climbed to rare heights. Brokers were euphoric. There were "go-go" stocks, "performance" stocks, "glamour" stocks. Touted by security analysts, traders, bankers, and brokers, McDonald's fitted right in with the circus atmosphere of the money mart. Wild optimism and glowing testimonials to growth swelled the value of the shares and, as speculators bid up the stock, more capital was provided to fire the grills and profits.

The noisiest trumpet at the exchange was McDonald's. Like a movie star, the "glamour stock" was surrounded with press agents who promoted it with Hollywood-style pizzazz. A high-powered public relations agency functioned as impresario. In 1965 it had orchestrated McDonald's debut on Wall Street with distribution of free hamburgers on the floor of the exchange. Further hype kept the name in the limelight. Press conferences announced new highs in earnings, statistics were released to demonstrate Big Mac's invincibility, gossip circulated that proclaimed McDonald's "invulnerable to recession," and all the while President Fred Turner, accompanied by a team of financial advancemen, stayed on the road, meeting with stockbrokers, market analysts, and shareholders. Little wonder that McDonald's was acclaimed the "darling of Wall Street."

The beefy star's most prominent endowment was "earning power." It was McDonald's share value on the exchange that excited investors. Each year McDonald's earnings rose by a startling 40 percent. This "growth" set investors panting. Fast food spelled fast money. The stock was snapped up by banks, insurance companies, pension funds—the most prestigious financial institutions. Wall Streeters unstintingly pushed the hot stock. The makers of hamburgers stood on the Exchange with the makers of steel, petrochemicals, electronics, computers, and technological future-gear. McDonald's ranked high alongside such institutional favorites as American Telephone, Polaroid, Sears, and Xerox. In fact, for speculative purposes, the hamburger shares were more appealing than IBM's or General Motors'; and the result was the same massive displacement of capital resources that took place in the twenties when speculators drove up stock, inflating it far beyond its worth. So McDonald's was only one among many to play the same kind of havoc on the market that had sent exchanges crashing in 1929. The preference of investors for hamburgers rather than steel was the microcosmic flaw of a financial system that invested vast resources in ground meat or the like rather than bolstering more vital sectors of the economy.

This parallel to the twenties was worrisome to Democratic Texas Senator Lloyd Bentsen, who warned in a 1974 speech that banks and other big financial institutions had wreaked chaos on the stock market by plunging huge amounts of money into a small number of securities. He charged that America's money masters had been buying the glamour stocks while ignoring the more solid companies. Bentsen specifically cited McDonald's as having, at the end of 1972, a book value of $200 million and a stock market value of $2.1 billion. U.S. Steel, by contrast, had a book value of $3.6 billion but a stock market value of only $2.2 billion at about the same time. "Something is wrong with our economy," the senator charged, "when the stock market is long on hamburgers and short on steel."

Bentsen's warning came as McDonald's stock was sinking to a new low. In a few years, the stock had aged and even its statistics became suspect. Two brokerage houses announced that they were dropping it from their recommended securities list, citing a saturated fast-food market, rising costs in food and labor, and a slowdown in profits. In February of 1973, when McDonald's was selling for nearly seventy dollars a share, Richard S. Bari of A. G. Becker and Company predicted that it would drop below forty. A year later, when Hamburger Central's rising menu prices no longer made its food a bargain, *New York* Magazine reported the brokerage house of Baker and Weeks also revealed that it had stopped advising clients to buy McDonald's because inflation would force the company's primary customers to economize. In the fall of 1974 the stock dropped to twenty-five dollars, reducing Kroc's $500 million fortune by nearly one third.

This came on the heels of a damaging article that suggested the glamour of the stock might have been mere tinsel, that the admirable earning record of America's fast-food giant was partially the result of some fast financial fudging.

The article, which appeared in *Barron's* financial journal, was by Professor Abraham J. Briloff, who accused McDonald's of misrepresentations in its financial statements. Briloff noted that "wherever ants swarm, the pot will contain a bit of honey, but also will be filled with accounting ploys," and he cited McDonald's as an example of how a company used these to show higher profits than were actually earned. Professor Briloff charged "major distortions," which Hamburger Central's "most prestigious auditors failed to reflect or at least disclose." There appeared to be less to the magic margin of profits than met the eye. Financial filler made McDonald's burgers "more palatable than its accounts," according to Briloff.

McDonald's countered with an ad in the *Wall Street Journal* in which it challenged these allegations. Then in September, 1973, a *Time* magazine cover story showed a happy, smiling hamburger afloat over a Pop Art tableau of an American flag, bright Golden Arches, and a shiny McDonald's installation. The six page article was a virtual panegyric to the company's power entitled "The Burger That Conquered the Country."

The *Time* spread blithely corroborated all the legends McDonald's had fostered about itself, as well as adding a few.

Some of *Time*'s reporters, who had swarmed out to cover Big Mac in various parts of the country, expressed their dismay. One San Francisco-based *Time* investigator found the story even harder to swallow than the hamburgers he had consumed in the course of his assignment. He had spent ten days covering many of the seventy Bay Area McDonald's outlets and emerged with an altogether different picture.

He had listened to youngsters complain about the company's iron control in the outlets, and he had heard union leaders denounce McDonald's for depressing pay levels throughout the restaurant industry. He had watched minority neighborhoods battle to keep McDonald's out of their communities, and had seen the high-powered squads of lawyers and lobbyists effect the conquering burger's advance through the courts after all other methods had failed. In the end he had formed a general impression of the hamburger System:

"Basically, I suppose, McDonald's is the epitome of capitalism—a success story built on shabby business practices; McDonald's is a morally corrupt organization that is not doing anything illegal."

Particularly vivid to him was an uncomfortable sense of suspicion, distrust, often outright paranoia, on the part of the McDonald's managers and franchised operators he had encountered. They had struck him as staunchly xenophobic, leery of any who were not "hamburger people." They obeyed a military-style chain of command, and during his visits they stayed in close touch by telephone with their regional commanders.

The hamburger overseers appeared to be bound to silence in discussing even the most mundane aspects of their operations, their duties, the System. They were all serious, intent young men with a striking similarity in attitude: "McDonald's puts them through their training program and now they're making all this money. They have convinced themselves that they're hot-shot entrepeneurs and super-salesmen when what they're really only doing is running a bunch of kids."

Hamburgerology
at Hamburger U.

"It Gets So Your Blood Turns to Ketchup"

Despite its idyllic name, Elk Grove Village is a busy pulsing cell in heartland America. It is ringed by broad, coursing expressways and an angry, rumbling sky. O'Hare International, the world's busiest airport, is nearby, and Chicago can be seen twenty miles distant.

The town is part of a dense, tristate area known by its 10 million people as "Chicagoland." Herds of elk used to roam here amid the groves. But the groves vanished and in their place came farmhouses, then bright clusters of roadside life: gas stations, motels, eateries, machine shops, apartment buildings, and long rows of warehouses. The elk vanished, too, of course, and in their place came herds of salesmen with samples and order books. In Elk Grove they stopped, showered, and shaved, and dreamed of commissions, promotion, advancement, success.

It was just such a group of men who gathered here one

brisk September day in 1968 for a little-noted ceremony. Foremost among them stood Ray Kroc and Fred Turner. The group had gathered around a hole in the ground. The bronze plaque was already in place beside it. A roar shook the skies from O'Hare, and a time capsule was lowered: a steel cylinder containing newspapers, annual reports, reams of hamburger statistics and commemorative coins. It would be opened again in 2010.

Quietly several of the men worked the earth back with shovels. There it was.

Hamburger University.

The building gleamed. It was brand-new and white, with a Moorish entrance and a bulbous glass well protruding from it. A thickly carpeted staircase could be seen winding to a circular skylight.

It was as Kroc had predicted back in '56. McDonald's had become a System that covered the country, requiring specially trained cadres—managers, assistant managers, crew personnel, field inspectors, regional, subregional and area supervisors. Unskilled people could be trained and relied upon to follow the Formula; could be instructed in the making and serving of a hamburger; in food preparation, equipment maintenance, purchasing, personnel, quality control; in advertising and community relations; in dealing with customers, crews, and unions; and in Kroc's founding principles.

Fred Turner had taught and systematized the body of knowledge now raised to the status of "Hamburger Science," as Kroc liked to call it. As early as 1961 he had established an "underground university" in Elk Grove Village that became known as the "pit" since it was held in the cramped, windowless basement of a local McDonald's stand. The first class to graduate from the pit totaled three students. After awarding the first Bachelor degrees in Hamburgerology, a dean was installed and the curriculum expanded. Facilities were added, professors, even scholarships, until there grew a need for a

more thorough educational complex, complete with seminars
and a postgraduate department, research grants, and a foreign
student program.

The time capsule carried the details of meeting these needs
in the founding of Hamburger University. And now it was a
reality.

Shortly after opening its doors in the fall of 1968, a blond,
blue-eyed, and affable young man appeared in the orange-
carpeted halls of Hamburger U. His name was Donald Breitkreutz. He was married, in his mid-thirties, with three young
children, and like Fred Turner, as well as most other members
of McDonald's management, he had been forced to drop out
of school at an early age.

Donald Breitkreutz began his career wrapping butter and
washing milk bottles in Wisconsin. After working his way up
to a sales route in dairy products, he became a stockboy in a
supermarket where he volunteered for a management training
course. In May, 1966, he joined McDonald's, first as a store
manager, then as a regional training supervisor for forty-eight
stands in the Washington, D.C., area. He helped open store
849 and was sent on to Elk Grove Village for further training.

At the time of Breitkreutz's arrival, Hamburger U still com-
prised the original wing. Classes were held once a month,
attended by a total of thirty-five students. There was a staff of
three. "And sitting there in the classroom," Donald Breitkreutz
recalls, "it somehow became a personal goal that someday I
would come back as a prof at Hamburger U."

A little over three years later, Donald Breitkreutz moved his
wife and daughters from Virginia to Illinois. In March, 1972,
Hamburger Central wanted him in Elk Grove Village. They
wanted him as a professor.

Donald Breitkreutz taught for nine months. He got a kick
out of teaching. He liked it better than his previous job as field
inspector, which involved constant travel over a territory that

ran from Dover, Delaware, to Ashland, Kentucky. Hamburger U allowed him to go home at night to prepare lectures and correct exams. He liked the exchanges in the classroom, the stimulating environment of fellow hamburgerologists. In the latter part of 1972 a shakeup took place at the Elk Grove complex and Donald Breitkreutz was hurriedly called in from the classroom to find himself suddenly installed as the ninth dean of Hamburger U.

The man who appointed him to the post was Jim Lynch, a vice-president and director of training, reputedly the only person among the highly charged Hamburger Central crew whom "you had to run to keep up with." Shortly after Donald Breitkreutz had moved into the dean's office, Jim Lynch called a meeting of HU's four-man staff in the think tank of Hamburger Central. Sprawling on the gently-rocking waterbed, enclosed by the soundproof conical-shaped walls and soothed by the soft musical tones emanating from hidden speakers, the men discussed the general goals and objectives of the school.

It was agreed that the professorial ranks of HU were not to become a dumping ground for people for whom McDonald's could find no other use. Up until Dean Breitkreutz's administration, a person could qualify as a "professor" after having worked as an assistant manager at one of the company's hamburger stands. Almost half the previous deans had completely dropped from view. Some had stopped practicing hamburgerology altogether. Jim Lynch, himself a former dean, decided that the staff had to be upgraded by instituting stiffer criteria.

Jim Lynch was Fred Turner's age. Like Turner, he had grown up with the System and become a millionaire. Suddenly, a few months after the think tank meeting, he got married and outfitted a new yacht for an indefinite sojourn in the South Pacific. When he bid good-bye to Dean Breitkreutz at Hamburger U, he said, "I have the dollars now to find out a little more about Jim Lynch."

Dean Breitkreutz stayed at Hamburger U and oversaw a

rapid expansion that more than doubled HU's facilities in a few months' time. Classrooms were added, walls ripped out. The design of HU's new staff quarters followed the open-office concept of Hamburger Central. There were plants, TRMs, mottoes, open movement, and free circulation of ideas. At times a half-dozen professors were exchanging thoughts, or listening to audio tapes, using slides and equipment, preparing lectures. Dean Breitkreutz fled to the one remaining office with a door. But in time, like everyone else in the McDonald's hamburger realm, Breitkreutz adapted to the open office and even learned to spurn people who still desired doors and walls. In his eyes General Motors is simply "an old stodgy company that still believes in private offices for its executives."

The dean is adorned with the Golden Arches—on his yellow shirt and green blazer pocket, on his tie and cuff links, on his attaché case. There are few books in his office, most prominently *I'm OK—You're OK*. An intercom on his desk allows him to listen in on every class. Each day he takes home Hamburger Central's top secret *Insight* bulletin lest it fall into unauthorized hands.

"I think McDonald's is unique," he says, with his wide-open, innocent smile, his feet propped on his desk. "The majority of its people have the same philosophy toward the hamburger. That is, it is not a joking matter to us, but a damn serious business."

His current staff reflects the growing stature of Hamburger U: two assistant deans, a senior professor, and four full professors. "They don't all necessarily have a college degree," Dean Breitkreutz acknowledges. "Some of them don't even have a high school degree. But this is McDonald's management teaching McDonald's management."

The individual zeal of the staff members makes the dean's meaning clear. When Ken Clement, one of the two assistant deans, gets behind the Snap-Action Grill he jumps up and down, talks fast and loud, and virtually electrifies the room. The other assistant dean, a Boston French-Canadian named

Jerry Pelletier, used to work for Friendly's Ice Cream and in a Pratt and Whitney plant. Pelletier maintains that it is possible to get addicted to hamburger. "I could eat hamburgers three times a day," he says raptly. "It gets so your blood turns to ketchup."

When Ray Kroc first began selling hamburger licenses, he preached the secret of small-business happiness: "We give people an opportunity to get into business for themselves without taking the whole risk alone. All we ask is that they follow our way of doing things, *the proven way*."

Initially, the proven way was taught primarily to new franchisees—aspiring small businessmen with the means to put down a sizable license fee. These were known as "owner-operators" and included lawyers, dentists, retired military brass, aerospace engineers, a professional football player, a former undersecretary of the navy, and even a chief steward knighted by the Swedish king. But in recent years, fewer and fewer licensees have been appearing at Hamburger U. A typical class in December, 1973, had no more than five out of a total of eighty.

The decline of owner-operators among HU's enrollment reflected McDonald's aggressive "buy-back" policy. Old franchise-holders were bought out and more and more company-owned stands constructed. With their higher profitability and more centralized control, the day appeared not far off that McDonald's would be a full-fledged chain-store operation, having eliminated completely the need for licensees whose initial capital and labor had produced the company's phenomenal growth.

McDonald's future expansion seems more contingent on its ability to nurture a steady supply of managers than it is on increased volume and acquisition of more stores. The owner-operator with an average annual income of $50–$70,000 represents, in effect, a *high*-paid manager for the duration of his twenty-year license, even though he frequently does the work of two and is often assisted by other family members. Essentially, the manager's function at a McDonald's stand consists of supervising a crew of high school kids performing simple, elementary tasks, and under Hamburger Central's guidance this expertise is quickly and thoroughly acquired.

The few licensees at HU can generally be distinguished by their older, more prosperous look, while the majority of students are in their late twenties and early thirties, with families, often with a string of factory, sales, or odd jobs behind them. They are the victims of a tight labor market and a lack of skills and education. At HU their first impression is one of sophistication and expense showered on what used to be the lackluster trade of hashslingers and short order cooks.

Hamburger Central prides itself on "weeding out" its managers "before they get behind the counter," and the minimum admission slip to HU is a six-month stint at a hamburger stand in the field. The lucky candidate for HU is told that he will be trained as a "professional manager," while the school prospectus informs him of his prestigious status: "In most companies, a degree from Harvard or Stanford or M.I.T. would be enough, but to the McDonald's people you really haven't proven you're management material until you've made it through Hamburger University."

Once enrolled, the students are admitted to what McDonald's calls "a rather elite and diverse group"; that is, "new licensees who've just joined the McDonald's family, and managers and assistant managers vying to make their mark on the competitive but promising corporate ladder." They quickly learn to speak of President Turner as "Fred," and of the chairman as "Ray."

McDonald's educational complex is not unique in the franchise industry, which is replete with almost as many training schools as there are trademarks, ranging from automotive workshops to a speed-tufting program taught aboard the *Queen Mary* in the port of Long Beach, California. The franchisor, writes Boston attorney Harold Brown in *Franchising: Trap for the Trusting,* "inculcates the franchisee with the necessity of being taught, guided and controlled not only during the initial training period but throughout the existence of the franchise." Training facilities are therefore particularly important among the fast-food/hotel franchisers, with their dependence on a set of standardized operations as well as a carefully indoctrinated attitude of service and loyalty. There are the no-nonsense classrooms of Mr. Donut in Massachusetts, Burger Chef's recently opened academy in Reston, Virginia, and KFCU (Kentucky Fried Chicken University) in Louisville, Kentucky. The Marriott hotel chain's food-training operations are headed by an executive from Procter and Gamble, considered a giant at devising management methods. The success of the fast-food franchise chains depends on the widest dissemination of management skills to thousands of people who have never managed a business before.

In 1970 the Holiday Inn chain, which is to hotels what McDonald's is to fast food, opened its own university in Olive Branch, Mississippi. Modeled closely after IBM's training program, Holiday Inn called its facilities a Learning Center featuring "total immersion" training. Something similar awaits the freshman at McDonald's Hamburger U, which claims that by the time "students earn their Bachelor of Hamburgerology, they're not only connoiseurs of the hamburgers, but the letters QSC are indelibly etched in their minds."

Each month, HU offers two classes simultaneously, turning out about one hundred and fifty hamburgerologists. Some seven thousand graduates have earned their degrees since HU's founding, and about two thousand were expected to graduate from the expanded facilities in '75. The programs offered are the two-week B.O.C. (Basic Operators Course) and the eleven-day A.O.C. (Advanced Operators Course). Classes begin promptly at 8:30 A.M., Monday through Saturday. After the third day, each class starts off with an exam on the previous day's material. And in the evening, long after the day's schedule is done, students linger in the open faculty office to ask professors questions, or gather in the equipment room to examine more closely cutaway models of McDonald's machinery.

Upon arrival at HU, the students are rapidly acquainted with the depth of their field. Their main text is the 360-page Operations Manual, which details everything from where to buy Ronald McDonald watches to how to scrape a grill and post a double ledger. Divided into three parts—Food, Equipment, and Management Techniques—the curriculum traces the patty-production line.

HU's varied menu of courses includes entrees like "Buns," "Filet/Steamers," "Carbonization," "Orange Bowl," "Fries/ Shortening," and "Beverage Electives," along with side readings on "Big Mac," "Quarter Pounder," "Shakes," and "Hot Apple Pie." Lectures range across a wide variety of topics. Students are instructed to recognize the "Five Enemies of Shortening" and to combat premature shortening breakdown. They study "Basic Refrigeration" and "Frozen Product Care," "Management Decision Skill," "Competition," "Building Maintenance," the dreaded "Teen-age," and the all-important "Cash Control." Precision is the key virtue stressed, and the students must not waiver from the standard prescriptions of McDonald's "recommended yield" for each product used in the store.

The practical side of the program finds the students learning the Multiplex Beverage System, the Taylor Shake Machine and Keating Fryers, the grills, toasters, and computerized french-fry system. There are, as well, regular workshops on heating, ventilation, air conditioning, grill calibration, and water filters. HU even boasts a "laboratory" that consists of an actual McDonald's stand located about a mile from the campus. And each day the students are tested on how to sanitize equipment, on food-product ingredients, shelf life, and cooking time, and on every other aspect of the manual.

Among the advanced courses available at HU are postgraduate seminars on such topics as real estate, law, reinvestment, financial analysis, and marketing. Guest speakers occasionally address these students on specialized areas of interest, such as labor relations, insurance, consumer research, and store promotions.

The conversation among postgrads rarely concerns hamburgers. During recess, they group in small bunches amid different portraits of Ronald McDonald in HU's bright yellow basement rec room, murmuring the jargon of property and law—of "left turns into the lot" and "deceleration roads"; of "building inspectors" and "evidences of title"; of "options on property" and "signed contracts" and "approval of curb rights."

Among the profusion of courses there is one area that is conspicous by its total absence—even though it is a question that most directly affects the patty-consuming public the managers are taught to "serve." Professors do not mention this subject; students fail to bring it up. It's a sensitive area, rife with controversy and best left alone. Hamburgerologists, like Augustinians, are not expected to question the attributes of the Patty Paramount, the hamburger *substance*—what it is made of, what it contains, whether it brings proper nourishment to the people. But to nutritionists, physicians, dieticians, and consumer crusaders, the subject has been less sacrosanct.

"The typical McDonald's meal—hamburgers, french fries, and a malted—doesn't give you much nutrition," charged Dr. Jean Mayer, professor of nutrition at Harvard University's School of Public Health, in a *New York Times* Magazine piece in July of 1974. "It's very low in Vitamins B and C, but very high in saturated fats. It's typical of the diet that raises the cholesterol count and leads to heart disease." Long-range health problems have been cited as the possible result of a regular diet of McDonald's-style junk food. Dr. George Christakis, nutrition chief at New York's Mount Sinai School of

Medicine, warned in a speech to the American Public Health Association against a future horde of debilitated Americans— "the McDonald's generation"—fueled by such fare. Allowing a youngster to join this generation, said Dr. Christakis, "can set the stage for chronic disease later in life," because by the time these youngsters reach fifty, one third of them would be high-risk heart-attack possibilities due to high cholesterol levels. "We must change our hamburger-malted way of life or change the content," urged Dr. Christakis. On the other hand, *Time* quoted Dr. Mayer as being "nonfanatical about McDonald's. As a weekend treat, it is clean and fast."

On a tour of McDonald's hamburger world, *New York Times Magazine* writer Anthony J. Lukas noted the most prominent characteristic of McDonald's basic machine-stamped patty—"precious little meat" but a lot of what people in the trade call "fixins." Since then the meagerness of meat has passed into national folklore as a standard gag. When Howard Cosell on the *Sonny and Cher Show* asked Chuck Connors, playing the owner of the "McTavish" hamburger chain, whether his business had been affected by the meat shortage, the answer from "McTavish" was: "Oh, no. We sold over 12 billion. That represents nearly nine pounds of meat."

"Big Mac," in particular, seems a mountain of "fixins" on a molehill of meat. With its formidable appearance and saber-rattling "Secret Sauce," it was truly the paper tiger of hamburgers. According to one *New York* magazine food critic, Big Mac was made up of "all those disreputable things—cheese made of glue, Russian dressing three generations removed from the steppes, and this very thin patty that is close enough to meat." A writer for *Today's Health,* taking a comparative sample of fast-burger brands, also gave Big Mac lowest marks, reporting that the "whole thing tasted like a charcoal-broiled roll garnished with day-old salad."

Bruce Hannon, an engineer at the University of Illinois, did an environmental impact study when the company was only half its present size. It was published by the *San Francisco*

Examiner on November 12, 1972. Hannon's study charged that
McDonald's packaging constituted a phenomenal drain on
natural resources. It took the sustained yield of 315 square
miles of forest to keep McDonald's supplied with paper packaging for one year. The electrical power used was the energy
equivalent of 12.7 million tons of coal, or enough to keep the
cities of Boston, Washington, and San Francisco supplied with
electricity for an entire year.

Faced with a growing wave of such consumer criticism,
Fred Turner has defended McDonald's food by saying that
nobody eats it as a regular diet, but as it became clear that for
a lot of low-income and ghetto people the McDonald's menu
increasingly constituted the main course of the day, Turner
decided that the time had come for McDonald's to do a nutritional study of its own.

The project was undertaken by a reliable hamburgerologist,
an old friend of Ray Kroc's named Ed Trazeman, once di-
rector of research for Kraft in Chicago. According to Kroc,
Trazeman had acquired a number of McDonald's franchises in
Wisconsin, which he sold back to Hamburger Central before
accepting the research project. Cushioned by a $300,000 Mc-
Donald's grant, he set up shop at the Madison branch of the
University of Wisconsin.

Trazeman's findings did not differ from the chief criticisms
of nutritionists. The data was released without fanfare, but
its effect soon became visible. An ad campaign was launched
by Hamburger Central suggesting that the McDonald's menu
should be complemented by a diet of more vital nutrients
and vitamins. It came out with a television commercial
featuring Ronald and the Nutrients, a rock band dressed as
symbols for vitamins and minerals, to encourage children to
eat food from the basic nutrient groups every day, along with
their regular dose of McDonald's hamburgers and shakes. The
ads ran for only one month—December, 1973—since in January, 1974, a new federal labeling law was scheduled to take

effect under which McDonald's could no longer advertise specific nutritional values without putting accurate labels of ingredients and contents on each fast-food item.

Hamburger Central advised its own operators (in the company's *Insight* Magazine) not to draw attention to the question of nutrition, suggesting that because of the sensitive nature of advertising nutritional values, local efforts should be limited to Ronald and the Nutrients when available.

One of Hamburger U's most important departments is the section called Marketing Communications and Creative Services. Consisting of a series of open offices on the second floor, its function is to design, implement and monitor the multimedia training system used in class presentations. HU's faculty uses the latest in teaching aids, and the school itself has been described as an "audiovisualist's dream," complete with soundproof studio, control panels, a ten-man staff, and studio engineer.

HU boasts portable closed-circuit TV; a projection room for each large classroom; controls that can hold a full day of pre-set materials; two 8-by-8-foot screens in the larger classrooms for 16mm motion pictures; overhead projection for 35mm slides, and shelves of slides and films.

Its film room permits filming, and taping, called Communicans. Executives tape messages for regional offices and the McFactories in the field, officials from Hamburger Central, including Ray Kroc and Fred Turner, have come to tape welcome speeches, while others admit to using Communicans for no other reason than to see "how they come across on tape." Training films are also made here. Elsewhere HU's portable TV camera whirrs away at "on-the-spot" happenings in operating stores, while a closed circuit television system monitors every corner of the building itself.

Like the machine-cut patties, graduates are not expected to vary. A sizable library of training films produced by Mc-

Donald's Marketing Communications Department was to ensure further the standard quality of management material. For sole use at Hamburger U and by licensees in the field, the films have such titles as *A Lot of People Sell Hamburgers* (about teamwork), *Six Steps to Success* (with comedian Pat Paulsen), *What's the Matter with You People?* (crew morale), and *Tug of War* (showing the manager-supervisor relationship). Another series of management development films includes short features, such as *How to Conduct a Tour* (of a McDonald's stand!), and *Federal Laws Regulating Employment Practices and You.* Other film strips carry titles like *Big Mac, Everybody Sell, If You Want to Work Hard,* and *The VIP at McDonald's* (the maintenance man).

Each hamburgerologist, besides being a manager or assistant manager, was to carry "the brand and the breed of corporate loyalty," the "esprit de corps" that chairman Ray Kroc admired so much in Sears, Roebuck. And the HU complex has succeeded in instilling these qualities to a degree that *has* made the company's managerial caste the envy of the fast-food business. HU grads staff the ranks of chains like Sandy's, Hardee's, Bonanza Steak houses, and Burger King. According to Dean Breitkreutz, competitors even happily grab up McDonald's management rejects.

"General Foods took a bunch of goddamn *flour people*, says Dean Breitkreutz, "and I'm going to be very blunt when I say this—and tried to make them into *hamburger* people."

A bust of Ray Kroc stands in the richly carpeted lobby of Hamburger University, the back of the bronze head turned to the dark-tinted window and the reflecting pool outside. Between classes the lobby becomes the crossroad for students who gather in bunches, carrying their manuals like order books. At peak hours, the whole university takes on the look of a busy sales convention. The light from wheel-shaped chandeliers is subdued as the students mingle in a swirl of bold-colored sports jackets, patterned shirts, turtlenecks, blazers, suits and ties. They have come from all over the United States and they talk with the regional accents of Main Street America. They are in a hurry. For most, HU is the only hope for a career and possible job security. Well into the night they will cling to their manuals in the dormitory atmosphere of the Elk Grove Hyatt Chalet—"Survey. Question. Answer. Read and Hunt. Think it Over. Recite. Review. . . ."

The students cling to prescribed steps to take them through the maze of subjects that have grown in number as well as complexity. The Science grew up with the System, and the System today is no longer simply confined to the making and serving of a hamburger.

In the early years when classes were held in the "pit," it had been enough to know the fast-food fundamentals—Kroc's Trinity of Patty, Bun, and Secret Sauce. But today Hamburger Central is active in many areas of public life. It is busy in Washington, fighting for *sub*minimum wages and against wage and price controls. It deals with municipal zoning and permit bodies, with courts, judges, and councilmen in virtually every American community, and it is engaged in a struggle with organized labor.

By 1973 union strife in the McDonald's stands had reached the point where Hamburger Central found it necessary to implement a comprehensive campaign. At HU this led to the hasty institution of a brand-new field of study concerned with the psychological methods of managing McDonald's vast work force, 90 percent of which consists of low-paid students and part-time teen-age workers. HU's addition to the curriculum dealt with "motivation" and "communication." The name of the course: Personnel I.

"We are at the point now," Dean Breitkreutz says proudly, "of developing our managers beyond the hamburger knowledge that they already have." Much of this development is in the hands of Dr. Leroy G. Cougle, known among the faculty as "Doc" Cougle, HU's only *real* Ph.D. and a *real* professor of Business Management at the University of Wisconsin.

Doc Cougle explains that Personnel I teaches that the manager's success will be primarily based on how he deals with the teen-agers working in the stand, but before he can "motivate" the "kids," he must have a positive image of himself. He must think of himself as being somebody very special because he works for a highly successful company that sells more hamburgers than any other in the world. He must think of himself as being able to determine his own life and achieve his goals. Personnel I was designed to indoctrinate this "positive" attitude throughout the ranks of hamburger management.

"The point is," says Doc Cougle, "I can't start motivating you as a subordinate until I have some decent feelings about myself. In other words, if I feel very negative about myself, that negativism will transmit that to you, and it is very difficult for me to treat you as a normal producing, achieving human being. If I think that I'm a no-goodnik, it becomes very difficult for me to deal with you in a very positive way. So the first thing I have to do is to start thinking positively about myself. The McDonald's managers do think positively about themselves. They're a part of the leaders of the industry, there's no question about that."

How positively HU students think of themselves is tested in Personnel I with one of Doc Cougle's sentence-completions in which members of the class are asked to finish the sentence "I am."

They usually respond with self-addressed tributes like "I am achieving" . . . "I am successful."

"They all come through very positive," says Doc Cougle, "because they do feel good about themselves; whereas if you were to ask that same question of a bunch of industrialists or the people running Burger King, it would be my guess that you would not get that almost unanimous agreement that 'I-am-something-very-positive.' "

Doc Cougle has been chiefly responsible for bringing Personnel I to Hamburger U. He is thin, sandy-haired, with a sharp nose and quick, darting eyes. He likes to wear a tan sporty suede three-button jacket and new-looking desert boots. Besides teaching at the University of Wisconsin, he is also chief partner in Cougle and Associates, training and organizational development consultants of Waukegan, Illinois. Twice a month he travels down to Elk Grove Village to administer his "motivation and communication" course.

Doc Cougle believes in the open office and the open shop, and on the question of labor he functions as HU's primary teen-age theoretician. He has instituted the current rule among McDonald's management to no longer refer to the young hamburger workers as "kids" but as "people." Consequently, the increasingly bitter labor strife in the hamburger stands has been reduced to a "people" problem—a "failure to communicate and motivate," according to Doc Cougle. "I have never seen a union shop that deserves to be called a union shop," he says. He is pleased to confide that McDonald's, thanks to Personnel I, has unions "pretty well beaten down for now."

Among HU's more colorfully dressed faculty, Doc Cougle conveys the look of the solid academic, secure in the world of concept, abstraction, social engineering, and psychological tests. In his own low-key collegiate way he is not much different from the aspiring small businessmen and hamburger managers he teaches—a traveling salesman from academe with a sample book of attractive products: Fleischman's work in "leadership"; the "achievement orientation" of Algeris; Herzberg's "job enrichment principles" and "five basic motivators"; and last, but not least, the Transactional Analysis (T/A) techniques of Dr. Eric Berne and Dr. Richard Harris.

In 1973 T/A became the vogue at Hamburger U. Everybody, including the dean, carried a paperback copy of Dr. Harris's best-selling *I'm OK—You're OK*, a hybrid of Dr. Coué and Dale Carnegie, Billy Sunday and Sigmund Freud. Transactional Analysis had been founded by the late Dr. Eric Berne, who believed that people had been "programmed" from an early age; and he set forth the techniques by which the "program" could be switched and tinkered with, tuned and adjusted.

Dr. Berne proclaimed T/A as a form of self-therapy to achieve a positive life-style and material success. But corporate management from Pan American to McDonald's, have found T/A useful in teaching supervisors the psychological techniques of handling their subordinates. One of the chief T/A techniques is called "stroking"—that is, giving signs of "recognition" and even "physical touch" in order to prompt other people's behavior and make them act in desired ways. An article in *Supervisory Management,* published by the *American Management Association,* recognized "stroking" as an effective "management tool." According to the article, a supervisor could use this technique in dealing with subordinates "in order to motivate, reward, or reprimand them."

Doc Cougle was instrumental in bringing T/A to Hamburger U as part of the "management techniques." "Most of the people we have working for us," he explains, "are high school youngsters, male and female. They're adolescents and they're searching and they're looking, and one of the things they search for is their own identity."

Personnel I expounds the labor crisis and T/A resolves it. HU's eager corps of graduate hamburgerologists is encouraged to motivate crews "by trying to find out what the individual needs are and trying to deal with them." Says Doc Cougle, "If that need is for recognition, then try to give that individual crewman recognition. A slap on the back, just saying hello is sometimes enough."

Commencement exercises for the graduates are held in the East Room at Hamburger Central, where they are presented with parchment degrees to mark their passage into the System—the B.H. (Bachelor of Hamburgerology) and M.H. (Master of Hamburgerology); also the Golden Hat for the student voted most helpful to his classmates, the Archie Award for the top man in the class, and a Parker pen that flashes "Quality-Service-Cleanliness" when the plunger is pushed, for outstanding seminar students.

6

Mac Under Attack

"It's 150,000 Kids Busting Their Tails Out There That Makes Us Tick"

Through the spring of 1973, one of New York City's most hallowed institutions found itself under siege. For almost two months, some five hundred men and women, mostly blacks and Puerto Ricans, picketed all six outlets of the city's famed Nathan's hot-dog chain. Complaining of "the lowest wages possible," the strikers paraded with signs and discouraged customers from entering. Nathan's countered by hiring "scabs" and increased its security personnel. Soon the familiar fast-food parlors took on the appearance of paramilitary encampments. There were scuffles and skirmishes, particularly at the Nathan's restaurant in Greenwich Village, where police finally waded into the line of picketers, jostled a few, and arrested seven.

The struggle at Nathan's was anxiously noted by other fast-food outfits. All of the successful chains depended on rock-bottom wages. Cheap labor was the basis for their extraordinary profits—lean pay and fat earnings. As the fracas at Nathan's made abundantly clear, the soft spot in fast food was behind the counters and in the kitchens. Only farm laborers and domestics earned less than the workers who grilled, fried, wrapped, and served the national quick-meal menus. Working conditions in the fast-food parlors were just as notorious. Employees were subject to arbitrary shifts, long hours, drudgery, and constant pressure from both managers and customers. Not surprisingly, the turnover rate in restaurants hit 300 percent a year, and by the early seventies labor strife was common throughout the industry.

The crisis first surfaced in 1968. Suddenly the cheap labor that was vital to the restaurant trade appeared to have vanished. Restaurants of all types, from Mom and Pop shops to the opulent shrines of *haute cuisine*, were suddenly faced with a shortage of cooks, countermen, and dishwashers. *The Wall Street Journal* blamed it on "the increasing reluctance of Negroes to take menial jobs," and the situation grew so desperate that one Marriott Hot Shoppe executive moaned he would consider hiring the "mentally retarded, physically handicapped, anyone." Noting that the industry should employ four million people by 1975, a director of the National Restaurant Association wondered where they would come from. Various suggestions were made, but none dealt with the central problem of low pay and bad hours.

A series of strikes compounded the labor troubles. For a good many establishments it meant folding up altogether after finding that they were unable to compete with the rapidly spreading franchised restaurants and fast-food chains. The process could be observed in most American cities as more and more neighborhood restaurants gave way to one of the nationally known parlors.

The key to the sweeping success of the fast-food chains was their low-cost labor and their almost exclusive reliance on part-time teen-age workers. McDonald's did not draw its employees from the general pool of culinary labor—much of which was unionized.

McDonald's, along with its fellow members of the International Franchise Association, pays the federal minimum and subminimum wage. Union rates are nearly double that, but paying even this essentially modest amount would spell disaster for earnings and profits. Harvard Business School professor Theodore Levitt described McDonald's in the *Harvard Business Review* as "a machine that produces, with the help of totally unskilled machine tenders, a highly-polished product." But regardless of the machine's reputed efficiency, the vaunted "automated kitchen" employs no less than fifty to eighty workers in part-time shifts.

The functions of the young workers are simple and monotonous. Ray Kroc's production-line approach broke down the older restaurant skills and made them into routinely mechanical operations. The "machine" could be sped up or slowed down, as the volume required. Significantly, its peak hours coincided with the hours youngsters were free to work—after school and on the weekends.

At Hamburger Central, the use of these young people is defended with the ring of economic and charitable virtue. McDonald's P.R. firm of Cooper and Golin has claimed that many of McDonald's part-time employees are "working to finance their educations or to supplement their family income." Chairman Kroc, a staunch promoter of the teen-age work ethic, sees a youngster's stint at McDonald's as a building block in the free-enterprise character. He is also the company's most openly outspoken enemy of organized labor.

"The unions haven't been able to touch us with a ten-foot pole," he says, proudly. "Hell, we got employees going to football games, basketball games, track events, hockey games. We have picnics for them. We have theater parties. We have softball games and on and on."

Not surprisingly, the AFL-CIO Culinary Workers Union

locals have long criticised the company for depressing wage
levels throughout the industry. Restaurants paying union
wages and for employee benefits, have long been opposed to
McDonald's, accusing it of unfair competition and exploitative
wage rates. Union locals across the country have tangled with
the hamburger colossus, and labor people cynically dismiss
Ray Kroc's paternal concern for his toiling teen-agers. "That
son of a bitch has been robbing every kid in the country,"
fumes Paul Meister, a veteran AFL-CIO union organizer in
Los Angeles.

Burly, graying, and jovial, Meister has nearly a quarter-
century's experience.

Meister does grant McDonald's one thing. He has seen the
battle of labor change. The opponent has grown sophisticated.

"You've got a different breed of cat now," he says re-
flectively. "McDonald's is *advanced*."

The bitter struggle at the Nathan's hot-dog chain in New
York showed the pitfalls of bosses doing battle with employees
fighting to organize themselves as a collective bargaining body.
Typically, the strike had been sparked by the firing of ten
black and Puerto Rican workers for alleged "union activity."
With "scabs," pickets, and police in daily turmoil, trade fell
off drastically. Battling small groups of angry men and women
did little to enhance the name of New York's famed hot dog.

Hamburger Central understood this lesson, and it turned
much of the question of combating labor into a matter of
public relations. Having police deal with striking workers was
not the way to solve labor disputes. It hurt the image, and
nothing at McDonald's was more valuable than the intangible
public facade that it had erected with inordinate energy and
vast sums of money expended in over two decades. McDonald's employees were integrally part of the picture that Ray
Kroc fondly likened to "a combination YMCA, Girl Scouts,
and Sunday school."

The young hamburger workers were expected to conform to rigid standards of grooming, courtesy, and behavior. "At McDonald's, personal appearance is something we watch every day," declares the manual. "A man should shave every day, clean his fingernails every day, keep his teeth and breath fresh and clean all the time, bathe often to prevent underarm and other body odors and use a deodorant. He should have dark pants, black shining shoes, a neat haircut and a clear complexion." The manual also laid down the specific character of the frontline McDonald's employee: "Personnel with bad teeth, severe skin blemishes or tattoos should not be stationed at service windows," it said, adding, "Your windowmen and outside order-takers must impress customers as being 'All-American' boys. They must display such desirable traits as sincerity, enthusiasm, confidence and a sense of humor."

But this code had been framed in the fifties, when labor militancy of after-school workers was unheard of. Things changed in the next decade as the issue of long hair was replaced by more serious disgruntlement—pay, working conditions, and excessive management control.

The discontent grew and in 1972, for the first time on a large scale, McDonald's crews began talking of organizing themselves into collective bargaining units, although Hamburger Central had earlier created a secret apparatus that was to prevent the discontent from reaching the confrontation stage.

In line with its customary low profile, Central theoretically fights no union battles. The company has long maintained that it would agree to unionization but that the workers are better off without a "third party" to come between crews and management. Economically, McDonald's argues that it is forced to pay rock-bottom wages in an industry where this is the rock-bottom rule. It says, not unjustly, that it needs the cheap labor to stay competitive, and that this is part of the "economic reality." The apparatus it employs to resist its workers on wages and unionization usually handles labor with a kid glove rather than the naked fist, having learned that manipulation is more effective than coercion. In Washington, McDonald's fights the battle with an effective *sub*minimum wage lobby, while internally its sophisticated antilabor apparatus roots out union sympathies from the ranks with propaganda, dossiers on organizing attempts, even lie detectors. But nothing compares to a combination bull session, psychodrama, and interrogation known to McDonald's young hamburger workers as the "rap."

The rap was born after President Fred Turner engaged the Chicago management consultant firm of A. T. Kearney to do a study and make recommendations. The conclusions of the Kearney Report startled everyone: There was nothing out in the field that stood in the way of McDonald's personnel and organized labor. McDonald's was wide open to union infiltration.

McDonald's apparently took the report very seriously. From the management consultant firm that authored these findings it hired away John Cooke, a former trade union organizer who had evidently changed his loyalties from labor to management. His close associate in this task was personnel director, Jim Kuhn.

Like Doc Cougle at Hamburger U, Kuhn believes in "recognizing" employees not as "workers" but as "people." "It's 150,000 kids busting their tails out there that makes us tick. I'm not a social worker. . . . If the unions succeed at McDonald's, then my job has failed."

A leprechaunish redhead, forty-year-old Kuhn holds an M.A. in industrial psychology and prides himself on an unorthodox, "human" approach to employment supervision. In response to the "needs of the kids out there," Kuhn gave them not only the rap, but also "recognition," "competition," "praise," and the "All-American Team."

Jim Kuhn designed the rap to show employees that Hamburger Central "cared." Theoretically, the employees registered their grievances while the hamburger manager listened. But in reality, the rap served an altogether different purpose.

Crews were encouraged to let off steam in a setting that appeared to be informal but was, in fact, highly controlled. They were given the privilege of "rapping" with the hamburger executives, with Jim Kuhn or any of his deputies in the field. The rap substituted talk for action and served to monitor the young hamburger workers.

The rap swung into action before the rumbles in the kitchens reached a boiling point. In effect, it was little more than a sophisticated interrogation technique. It was used whenever young workers attempted to organize themselves, as shown by Central's confidential report on union activities in the month of August, 1973. The report cites employees in La Grange, Illinois threatening union organization and rap sessions accelerated to determine the extent of union sympathy among the crew. Likewise, in Cahokia two crew members outwardly advocating union organizing, resulted in accelerated rap sessions to determine the extent of crew sympathy.

The rap was familiar to McDonald's management graduates, its elements having been studied in Doc Cougle's course. The technique adapted the tenets of Transactional Analysis, especially manipulative flattery and ego "stroking."

Jim Kuhn spread the teen-age gabfest concept to every stand. Managers and operators were given detailed instructions on how and where to hold such sessions and what to ask. Inside Hamburger Central, Kuhn assembled a staff of people to interpret and study the information collected and to guide their further development. The local raps led to regional raps, district raps, finally to a national rap, which saw hamburger workers being flown in from all over the country to participate. Jim Kuhn filmed the First National Rap Session.

"I'll brag about it. I think it's fantastic," says Kuhn. "I've seen it ten times and I still get tears in my eyes every time I watch it."

An important adjunct to the rap was recognition—"Recognition of the Employee as a Unique and Important Being." To Doc Cougle at Hamburger U, a teen-ager could be satisfied with as little as "saying hello," or a "slap on the back." But to Jim Kuhn at Hamburger Central "praise" was a prime catalyst in motivating workers and maximizing their productivity. He fought to dispel the idea that "fear-leadership" was the only way to get the job done. "It [praise] *will not* go to people's heads," Kuhn argued. "It *will not* take too much time. It *will* serve as a powerful example, not only to those receiving the praise, but to others who seek it. And it *will* bring a lot more fun to our day-to-day existence."

Along with the rap, recognition, and praise, Jim Kuhn introduced "competition" as a standard tool in the McDonald's management kit. Completion was a spur to greater output that took the normally dull and exhausting work of window people, grillmen, and others and made it into a game. "Competition," Kuhn wrote in a 1971 memo, "sets the tone for recognition. It is a strong motivational factor even when #1 is not present. Peer group pressure does the job."

The idea, as Kuhn was fond of saying, was not to create programs but to instill an "attitude." Competition was designed to transform the feelings of the hamburger workers toward their jobs and to deter them from acting collectively. As the youthful workers vied to outflip and outfry one another, the hamburger kitchens accelerated. It turned working for rock-bottom pay into a sport and the fastest and most efficient workers even gathered to compete for a place on McDonald's "All-American Team."

Created by Jim Kuhn, the competition held its first meeting in Las Vegas in 1972. The young hamburger workers flew in from all over to match their speed in stuffing bags of french fries and pouring Cokes. Scores and records were set at the "First National Hamburger Olympics." Participants were judged in such events as the number of Big Macs prepared in an hour, the fewest Cokes spilled, and the tidiest cash drawers. Pleased with the results, Hamburger Central advised that in presenting the awards, it "can be particularly exciting if the 'Oscar' winner technique is used."

In the fifties, one-liners attributed to Kroc in Chicago newspaper columns contained numerous cracks about youngsters who wrecked the family car, listened to Elvis Presley, or asked their parents for money. In the sixties, when cheap restaurant labor became scarce, Ray Kroc bemoaned the fact that parents spoiled their children, giving them everything they desired instead of letting them earn a few dollars at places like McDonald's. During a San Diego press conference he assailed the eighteen-year-old vote. "When I was a kid you weren't a man till you were twenty-one," he observed, "and the politicians are now giving beer to eighteen-year-olds. They let 'em vote, you know. What the hell! They won't know who they're voting for, *for ten more years!*"

However, Ray Kroc himself "recognized" young people by giving them McDonald's "All-American Band," which for the past seven years has selected two high school musicians from each state to march in the Macy's Thanksgiving Day Parade in New York and Rose Bowl Parade in Los Angeles. It was Kroc's way of "recognizing" "kids" who didn't rebel or fool around, Hamburger Central said.

The image of youngsters is engrained in the curriculum at Hamburger U under the special course called "Teen-age." *New York Times Magazine* writer Anthony Lukas reported having attended a class in 1971 during which a professor warned the students: "Watch out for teen-agers. They can definitely affect your profit picture by driving away your adults. They are extremely noisy and messy. They'll use profanity, and that can never be allowed at any McDonald's. They'll neck on your lot—and you better nip necking right in the bud." The professor also warned against the "really terrifying experience if you have two hundred or four hundred people descend on you for a rumble." He recalled that some managers had been badly injured in scuffles with the dreaded "teen-age," but the professor didn't recall any being killed.

Despite its sophistication and expense, the thorough apparatus to control the teen-age workers has not altogether functioned efficiently. No union has yet been able to enter the McDonald's kitchens, but neither has labor strife gone away. In 1973 it embroiled the company as never before. During a few weeks in October Hamburger Central's own report cited trouble at stands across the land, from Potsdam, New York, to Phoenix, Arizona.

Many of McDonald's franchisees found themselves caught in the middle. Having been unprepared for the struggle with labor, they were forced to protect their investment by bearing the brunt of Hamburger Central's battle.

As McDonald's ran into increasing resistance, the raps were accelerated, competition was increased, praise lavished more liberally than ever. But all across the country the hamburger workers were organizing themselves with a determination that became more embittered. At different stands workers called in safety inspectors, formed "gripe" committees, circulated petitions, passed out leaflets, and accused the company of using illegal tactics, including intimidation, inducements, and temporary benefits, to win union elections.

As a result of the growing militancy among its workers, Hamburger Central stiffened what it called "personnel practices which will help us maintain our non-union status." A steady stream of intelligence from the kitchens reached the open office of Jim Kuhn. Modishly dressed teen-aged assistants helped him interpret the news. According to Kuhn, his close associate, the fiery John Cooke, is "the best rapper I've ever seen." One of his more memorable speeches, according to one informant, occurred in the fall of '73, when the union struggle came to McDonald's Chicagoland stands. Appearing before Hamburger Central executives and owner-operators in

Chicago's Playboy Club, Cooke is said to have ominously warned that "the enemy was within."

It is doubtful, though, whether even the rap could have done much for McDonald's in the spring of 1972, when a number of leading citizens appeared in San Francisco's gray-stone City Hall.

They had come to testify before the five-member Board of Permit Appeals, the municipal body that reviewed new construction licenses. They were united in purpose. McDonald's threatened "to sabotage the whole economic situation in San Francisco," said their chief spokesman, Joe Belardi, executive secretary of the AFL–CIO Culinary Workers Union and president of the Labor Council. According to press accounts, he informed the board that the majority of the citizens opposed "the McDonaldization of San Francisco." Belardi pleaded with the board to void the construction license that had been approved for McDonald's a month earlier. The union leader reportedly characterized the hamburger chain as an "unfair competitor engaged in exploitation of young people for profit and personal gain," and he urged that it be henceforth banned from the city.

A number of other spokesmen backed up Belardi's appeal. Even the traditionally conservative Hotel Employers Association sent a representative to criticize the permit that would allow the McDonald's flag to be raised in San Francisco's scenic Marina District: "Any man has the right to compete in this city as long as he competes fairly. But to allow an organization like McDonald's to come in and scoop up the cream of the business without paying the going rate is not right."

A spokesman for Foster's West, a local cafeteria chain, told the Permit Appeals members that his company had decided not to renew a lease on a Marina District site where it had operated for forty years after hearing that McDonald's was about to move into the area. Foster's West paid its unionized employees double McDonald's wages. "We can't compete with this kind of competition," the representative complained. McDonald's own spokesman at the hearings, however, defended Central's belief that opening a store anywhere was "its true right."

San Francisco is a strong "union town," with a history marked by fierce labor struggles. It's a city in which the unions have won their rights dearly and where organized labor has long played an active role in local affairs. After listening to the witnesses, the board unanimously voted to refuse McDonald's the building permit. "I'm all for helping people get jobs," one of the board members was quoted as saying, "but not at $1.85 an hour. That's ridiculous. If McDonald's wants to come into an area like San Francisco, it should be made to meet the area's conditions."

The decision apparently hit Hamburger Central's most sensitive nerve and its response was massive. Everything it could muster was thrown behind its defense of the open shop. It used the courts, government agencies, and every legal technicality in the book. Ray Kroc himself joined the battle. Mayor Alioto intervened. The unions, the press, community groups, property owners, and restaurant associations plunged into the fray, and by the following year the San Francisco *Chronicle* speculated whether McDonald's had "concocted a hamburger that's almost too hot to handle."

Few newspapers outside San Francisco printed the amazing story of a city that for more than a year succeeded in withstanding the onslaught of "McDonaldization."* During this period hardly a week went by without another startling revela-

---

* One of the reasons that so few newspapers outside San Francisco printed the story might be found in the delicacy of the issue. Newspaper publishers, too, distributed their daily product the same way McDonald's distributed hamburgers. The system of newspaper distribution also sold franchises to district managers, who employed and managed thousands of news carriers even younger than the hamburger workers. The nation's newspaper industry used the same system of local distributorships that permitted avoidance of child labor and social security laws.

tion about the hamburger giant. Like the people in no other American city, San Franciscans saw the other face of Big Mac. They learned about the ire of the Hamburger King and the extremes McDonald's would go to. It was a shocking story of manipulation and showed the determination of a multibillion-dollar company to protect its vital source of cheap labor in a test case that threatened to set a shattering precedent for its operations elsewhere. The hamburger chain already had a history of troubled labor relations with the two stands it was then operating in the city. The first one had opened in August, 1971, in a multiracial neighborhood near San Francisco City College. A second stand appeared on downtown Market Street in February, 1972. Both had immediately become the scene of picketing and angry confrontations between culinary workers and burger brass. The pickets had been ordered stopped by the National Labor Relations Board in what was seen as a victory for Big Mac, but the rejection of McDonald's application for a third restaurant renewed the hopes of organized labor. In quick succession the Permit Appeals Board turned down Hamburger Central's applications for two additional sites, and by the end of the year full-page ads began appearing in San Francisco's two dailies. They were not really ads but "open messages" signed by Ray Kroc—open messages from the open office in defense of the open shop.

The Hamburger King criticized the labor unions and condemned them for filling young people's heads with dangerous notions. "The unions read the papers," he was fond of saying, "and find out that we're successful making money, and obviously doing a lot of business, and when you hire from fifty to a hundred employees per store, that's more than a restaurant hires; that's more than a supermarket hires."

Ray Kroc seemed to take San Francisco's resistance personally. In his open messages to the citizens of San Francisco he asked why the Permit Appeals Board was denying jobs to three hundred "of your city's youth." And, he asked, why San

Francisco was "denying us the right to free enterprise after we have complied with all your codes and regulations?"

In January, 1973, he filed an $11.1 million triple-damages antitrust suit against the Golden Gate Restaurant Association, the Hotel Employers' Association, and the San Francisco Joint Board of Culinary Workers, Bartenders and Hotel-Motel and Club Service Workers. Ray Kroc contended that labor officials and restaurant owners had "conspired" to pressure the Board of Permit Appeals into denying licenses for McDonald's outlets. "We filed this suit," Kroc was quoted by the *Chronicle*, "not only for ourselves but for the benefit of the San Francisco public who desire low-priced wholesome food, the McDonald's licensees who want to do business in San Francisco and students and housewives who are being denied the right to work." And he added that the labor officials and rival restaurant owners "knew" their opposition to McDonald's to be "a sham and frivolous."

McDonald's received support from other minimum-wage employers and even the prestigious *Wall Street Journal* rallied to Kroc's side in an editorial that criticized San Francisco for opposing McDonald's "right to free enterprise" regardless of any exploitation inflicted on its workers. "Yet somehow the argument about exploitation is hard to follow," the editorial noted sarcastically, "especially when one thinks of North Beach and other areas of San Francisco whose economies are built around nude night clubs and silicone celebrities. No doubt the performers are unionized. Still, somehow we can't see how a city . . . [doesn't] allow youngsters the choice of deciding whether they would be better off employed at $1.75 an hour or unemployed at union scale."

A few weeks after Ray Kroc launched his suit, McDonald's burst into the news again. This time the story raised eyebrows all over the city. The details came out of the testimony from a group of former McDonald's employees before San Francisco's Deputy Labor Commissioner, Bryan P. Seale. The young witnesses testified to personnel practices that offered a frightening glimpse of a Brave New Kitchen. During a Labor Division hearing lasting five hours they stated that employees had been forced to submit to lie-detector tests and that refusal was grounds for dismissal. While wired up, the witnesses said, employees were queried about union sympathies, and whether they had ever stolen or given away a hamburger. One of the specific questions asked was "Did you ever steal a minute of McDonald's time?" The ex-employees also charged McDonald's with taking tips and adding these to the restaurant's cash receipts.

Both the use of lie detectors and the appropriation of tips without notifying the public were violations of California's Labor Code. McDonald's spokesman at the hearing admitted the use of polygraph tests, but he denied that they were "forced." Employees were asked to submit voluntarily and refusal did not cost them their jobs, he said. Former employees, however, maintained that the management of the Market Street stand implied dismissal both by what it said and in the notices put on the shop's bulletin board. Another McDonald's manager simply defended the practice by saying that employees were asked the same questions with or without the lie detector during routine investigations of "problems" in the restaurant.

The question of "forced" polygraph tests remained a matter of conflicting testimony until it was solved—quite by accident—when Labor Commissioner Bryan Seale found a document in a pile of company bulletins and job application forms. The document was an old job application. Seale studied it closely and found a revealing paragraph above the applicant's signature—a few lines of fine print stipulating that each employee must acknowledge his obligation to take a lie-detector test upon request or face dismissal!

In his final verdict, Seale found against McDonald's on both charges and ordered the company to cease these practices or face court action. McDonald's use of lie-detector tests, he said, was in violation of state laws regardless of whether employees had signed a form giving their consent to such tests. The commissioner ruled that the consent forms "are obtained under real or fancied duress and coercion in that the employees believed that their hours of work would be reduced or that their employment would be terminated if they refused to 'voluntarily' consent. . . ." On the question of McDonald's appropriation of customers' gratuities, Seale found, "it is clear that employees are required to turn in all tips and that no records of these tips are maintained." He said there was no notification of the general public that the company kept this money.

A cease and desist order was issued. The holding was not appealed. Ray Kroc's suit, meanwhile, had been dismissed by the Federal District Court as not being within its jurisdiction.

Popular resistance against McDonaldization grew. Even Mayor Alioto, seemingly hungrier for labor votes than hamburger, pledged to defeat the process that threatened both the breadwinners who earned union scale and the small businessmen who had been in San Francisco for many years. While Big Mac hammered on the Golden Gate, Alioto, according to a union official, declared in a speech at a labor benefit in Minnesota that McDonald's would not be allowed to expand further in San Francisco unless it met the city's labor standards. During the speech Alioto is said to have revealed that pressure had been brought to bear on him from the highest hamburger quarter. Ray Kroc, he told the labor officials, had personally invited him over to a hotel and asked what it would take to put a third McDonald's in San Francisco. "That would take a union, Mr. Kroc" was the answer, Alioto said. The guests cheered and applauded.

Opposition reached a high point in the fall of 1973, after Hamburger Central filed suit in Superior Court to seek reversal of the Permit Appeal Board decisions that had kept it from building more stands in San Francisco. McDonald's had applied for sites in the city's low-income Mission District, but

the mainly Mexican and Latin residents made it immediately
clear that they did not want the open hamburger shop in their
community. "Fact sheets" were circulated explaining that
McDonald's would affect locally owned businesses that
catered to the ethnic tastes of the community. A drug program
director claimed that it would attract heroin pushers because
drug dealers liked to operate out of places like hamburger
stands. A spokesman for the Mission Senior Citizens denounced McDonald's for not hiring citizens over fifty-five years
of age.

The anti-McDonald's campaign in the district gathered
support from such groups as the Mission Coalition Organization, the Marina Property Owners Association, San Francisco
Tomorrow, the All Peoples Coalition, the San Francisco chapter of United Professors of California, the Student Council of
City College, the Haight-Ashbury Council, the Mission Rebels,
the Delancey Street Foundation, and other civic organizations.

"The basic issue is whether the people of San Francisco can
decide what types of businesses are harmful to our community
standards," said Joe Belardi of the Culinary Workers Union.

McDonald's pressed on against all opposition. To Hamburger Central the question of unions went to the heart of its
existence. The profits, the stock, the hamburger millionaires,
Hamburger Central, Hamburger U—everything stood like a
giant inverted pyramid on the pinpoint of minimum wages. If
stopped in San Francisco, it could be stopped elsewhere.

But in the end, not even San Francisco's united front could
withstand Big Mac. After nearly a year and a half of litigation,
pressure, and appeals in a series of cases that went from hearing to rehearing to continuance, from the lower to the higher
courts and to government arbitrators in Washington, Mc-
Donald's was finally issued a permit to build its stands in the
Mission District.

Law and order was on the side of McDonaldization. The
National Labor Relations Board declared, as it had in other

cities, that union elections could only be considered valid if held in McDonald's as one large unit, rather than in individual stands. In a similar vein, the superior court overruled the Permit Appeals Board after McDonald's found a section in the Municipal Code stipulating that the board's jurisdictional time to act on complaints against the company had run out.

The groups and organizations involved in the struggle against the hamburger giant could only express their frustration. But as the Golden Arches arose on Mission Street, none was more furious than the eighty-year-old vice-president of the board, Peter Boudoures, who shared Ray Kroc's belief in free enterprise, except that he took it to mean free competition with everyone paying the prevailing wage.

"Kroc is taking advantage," Boudoures kept saying. "McDonald's is after the almighty dollar, and they don't care about neighborhoods and how many small businessmen they ruin."

Having operated a restaurant that did a thriving business near City Hall for over thirty years, Boudoures was proud of the fact that he had always dealt fairly with his employees. He apparently considered himself a small businessman first and foremost, but he also recognized the rights of workers to union pay and benefits. He believed that McDonald's tremendous success had come at a high cost to many small businessmen, and so he was the company's most outspoken critic in the city chambers.

In semiretirement, Boudoures still ran a local savings and loan business. He was eight years older than the Hamburger King, and just as stubborn. He sat ramrod straight at the meetings of the permit board to which he had been appointed by Mayor Alioto, and he simply insisted that it just wasn't fair. "McDonald's takes advantage of the kids," he said. "McDonald's would be a detriment to the small people who have been here for many years."

Among his colleagues and in the press he earned the reputation of being "irascible." Boudoures rebutted that he had looked up the word and found himself in agreement with the definition—"prone to anger." McDonaldization made him irascible.

7

Advertise, Advertise, Advertise

"Early to Bed"

The wind snapped at the flags flying from the buildings; ropes contained the sidewalk crowds. Working men and women and their children all bundled up in their finest. The big department stores were closed, but the goods could be seen stacked high in the windows. The constant press of the throngs was kept back behind the sidewalk ropes by beefy cops on motorbikes. They kept the middle of State Street empty. Opposite the Big Mac bus, a platform had been raised, a grandstand lined with fold-up seats that were being occupied gradually by people who surveyed the street and the crowds with a proud, proprietary air.

The exclusive parking spot had been arranged in advance with the city. On this festive December day it functioned as a "hospitality center" for hamburger VIP's to watch Chicago's annual Christmas Day Parade, the city's grand event of the year.

Ned Locke, the traditional master of this ceremony for millions of TV viewers, would shortly go on the air from a choicer spot a few blocks down State. Meanwhile, in the luxurious lap of Big Mac, Ned chomped on an Egg McMuffin. McDonald's was sponsoring the broadcast.

The number of VIP's aboard Big Mac proved disappointingly small—mainly advertising and public relations lieutenants, the frontline contingent that had secured McDonald's hegemony over Chicago's Christmas Day.

The most notable figure was Ronald McDonald, sitting in front of a mirror console basting his face with white powder. His wild red wig hung askew over his ears. He straightened it and hopped down the aisle like a mechanism with an awkward spring. Then a door hissed and Ronald McDonald jumped from the bus. He cleared the sidewalk ropes and cavorted down State Street.

The first marchers appeared, led by a big-boned high school girl. She threw the baton high, straightened her back, one hand implanted on her hip. Ronald McDonald was suddenly frolicking through the ranks of the marchers. His baggy pants embroidered with golden arches on outsize pockets that flapped in the wind as he chased a high school student dressed in a striped shirt, a mask, and a flowing black cape. It was the Hamburglar, another of the stock McDonaldland characters.

Another band appeared; Ronald McDonald staggered between the brass tubas and the clattering cornets, while the Hamburglar pranced and skulked, weaving from one side of State Street to the other.

Ronald McDonald came to a stop directly before the grandstand and cast up a grimace. Mayor Richard Daley of Chicago waved an ungloved, chubby red hand.

Fleeting as it was, Ronald McDonald's salute to Mayor Daley had not come about by accident. Wires had been pulled to thrust this moment into the living rooms of millions of midwestern TV viewers. Weeks of preparation, phone calls, letters, memos, and invocations of important names in various city departments had smoothed the way for a barrage of McDonald's jingles, commercials, and special Yuletide exposures in other large metropolitan centers. Parades, plum pudding shakes, McDonald's gift coupons, and season's greetings: Christmas had been turned into a hamburger holiday.

The campaign to identify Christmas with the hamburger was one of Cooper and Golin's early undertakings. It began as early as 1959, when Chicago's news media described the arrival of the "Santa Wagon" in Chicago's downtown Loop. Behind the wheel was Ray Kroc, who personally distributed hamburgers and coffee to the Loop's jolly Saint Nicks and Salvation Army workers. The tradition was established. The story became a set piece in the local papers, a regular feature that linked the notion of Santa Claus with a chauffeur by the name of McDonald's.

The legend was enhanced later when Cooper and Golin propagated a touching Christmas story. It concerned a child who was asked where Mr. Santa had met Mrs. Santa. "At McDonald's," the child supposedly replied. This found its inevitable way onto the news wires and the papers across the country. Small towns in particular gave it the display of a prominent news item.

A few years later Cooper and Golin announced with even greater fanfare that 96 percent of American children were able to identify Ronald McDonald. This made the company clown a close second to Santa, according to Cooper and Golin. The data was attributed to a "Ronald McDonald Awareness Study." Again, the item made news all across the country.

But characteristically, nobody at C. and G. to this day knows *who* did the study. There is no record of the number of children sampled, their socioeconomic and racial backgrounds, or ages. Nevertheless, this lack of statistical basis did not stop the story from gaining widespread currency. The thirty-fourth edition of Ice Capades, for instance, pointedly paid homage to Ronald McDonald in an elaborate Las Vegas–style number as "a national figure second only to Santa Claus." "Maybe, very maybe," was the skeptical comment of *Los Angeles Times* entertainment critic Charles Champlin, who described the mixture of film and live skating as "a long, dumb commercial."

Statistics were Cooper and Golin's favorite propaganda tool in the early days of McDonald's and remained so during the company's growth. In 1961, when August was declared National Sandwich Month, McDonald's predicted that during this period it would put 7,000 miles of cheese on its cheeseburgers. Three years later, it announced the momentous news that hamburger was the favorite food of travelers. The sale of McDonald's first billion burgers was accompanied by the information that this total had been garnished with enough pickle slices to reach the height of the Empire State Building. On the occasion of the sale of the 6 billionth burger, it was revealed that a total of 460,938,356 pounds of flour had gone into the making of the buns, and that it would take 3,717 stripped-down 747 jumbo jets to haul the flour for these buns, while the ketchup and mustard for 6 billion patties was enough to fill the 46,770-gallon fuel tanks of 224 big 747's.

With the sale of the 12 billionth hamburger, Cooper and Golin illustrated how this total stacked in one pile would form a pyramid 783 times larger than that of Snefru. Greater London, it said, was the area required to accommodate all the cattle standing flank-to-flank that had gone into the making of the 12 billion. Then the ultimate: to consume them all, one man would have to eat a hamburger every five minutes for 114,000 years.

The original oracle behind these figures had been a gag writer by the name of Max Cooper. "He was a bad gag writer," his partner Al Golin would recall. After penning jokes for a number of aspiring comics, Max Cooper decided to open a public relations agency catering to clients with a penchant for wit. One of his first visitors was especially droll, and by the late fifties the Chicago papers began to blossom with corny one-liners attributed to a relentless jokester—unfailingly identified as "Ray Kroc (of the McDonald's drive-in-chain)."

For several years a weekly supply of *bon mots* attributed to the chairman and his hamburgers appeared in three principal Chicago columns: "Herb Lyon's Tower Ticker" in the *Tribune,* Irv Kupcinet's "Kup's Column" in the *Sun-Times,* and Nate Gross's "Town Tattler." Under Cooper's direction, the hamburger went vaudeville and Ray Kroc took the stage, assailing his reading audience with a barrage of gags that took the McDonald's name from the derisible to the highly visible.

The Hamburger King would also indulge his weakness for gags with visits to Chasen's, a celebrity hangout in Los Angeles, where he enjoyed trading lines with the likes of comedian Jack Carter and Sammy Davis, Jr. So Ray Kroc was pleased when Johnny Carson looked quizzically at his confrère Ed McMahon and said, "I just noticed McDonald's sold another pound of hamburger. They just flipped over the sign." Or when Bob Hope asked an audience at Notre Dame University whether the sign said "Thirteen billion served? Or thirteen billion saved?"

Max Cooper choreographed hamburger humor but, as business picked up, he became more serious. He ended up owning *fourteen* McDonald's franchises in Birmingham, Alabama.

While Max Cooper established his own small dominion within Kroc's empire, the agency fell in the hands of Al Golin, his junior partner. A mere twenty-six when he met Ray Kroc, Golin also came from a show business background. His father had been the owner of a theater chain, and in the early fifties Al Golin went to work for MGM as a road manager for such movie celebrities as swimming star Esther Williams and Clark Gable. Golin retained Cooper's vaudeville concept in promoting McDonald's, but he made the hamburger into a star by becoming its most zealous press agent—a master stager of pseudo events.

Al Golin breathed life into Mr. McDonald's and bestowed

the gift of speech, something called McLanguage. "McDonald's is McBest with McBest fries and delicious apple pies," Mr. McDonald's would prattle. The hamburger promoter counted in McMathematics, noting that children under seven years old ate 1.7 hamburgers per week; ages seven to thirteen ate 6.2; thirteen to thirty ate 5.2; thirty to thirty-five ate 3.3; thirty-five to sixty ate 2.6; and the aged over sixty ate 1.3 per week. Mr McDonald's "served" hamburgers—it did not "sell" them.

As the image took hold, its creator became a discreet and shadowy power. "We are not just your average PR firm," he would admit. Indeed, Al Golin sits on Hamburger Central's top steering committee; he accompanies president Turner to all important security analyst meetings; he was one of the chief forces behind the founding of Hamburger U. As the invisible hand that bids the hamburger to sit up, speak and be noticed, the impact of Golin's work even reaches Wall Street.

It was on Main Street America that Al Golin found the cheapest and most effective way of keeping the hamburger name in the limelight. In each locale, Mr. McDonald's was urged to join the Chamber of Commerce, the school board, United Way, American Legion, or other civic group, and any legitimate charity that came along. Thus the hamburger persona became a defender of the middle-class norm, a promoter of established virtue, a resister of change, and a welder of conformity.

As a reward, McDonald's would give out a free hamburger. Students in Wisconsin could turn in the A's on their report cards for a hamburger. In Indiana, any child who brought in his grandparents received an "All-American Meal"—hamburger, french fries, and shake. There were hamburgers for firefighters, good citizens, and anti-litterbugs. But strangest of all was the news account of a police chief in Pottsgrove, New Jersey, who announced that his force would start pulling over *safe* drivers at the behest, it was revealed, of McDonald's, which wished to reward good driving with a coupon for a free snack.

Under Golin's direction, Mr. McDonald's could be seen grandstanding during such events as a "Ladies Litter Pickup" in Johnson City, Tennessee; at a "Lite-a-Bike" program in Fort Worth, Texas; during a Beautification Week in Oceanside, California; at a "Clean the Desert" day in Las Vegas; and at hundreds of other civic and charitable functions all over the country. On Flag Day, Mr. McDonald's would fly more flags than anyone. He would also outfit Boy Scouts for a battle to "Save Our American Resources." During the Apollo moon landing program it came out with moon maps and, when nature conservation rode high, schoolteachers across the nation were offered McDonald's own Ecology Action Pack.

Cooper and Golin would regularly forward detailed lists to Hamburger Central with pointers on how to milk a variety of local events for promotional mileage. Typical of its expectations from these activities was the epilogue to a fund-raising drive for the Kansas City Zoo, which Mr. McDonald's led, in conjunction with a Triple Ripple Ice Cream promotion. This campaign received "not only press coverage and television exposure," the franchisees were duly informed, "but also generated a great amount of community goodwill in the area."

It was in the thousands of communities across the land that Al Golin discovered the rich lode of virtually free media exposure that helped make McDonald's a household word. All the refinements of press agentry were marshaled in this mission. One advertising account executive who manages a McDonald's account described the strategy as "participatory public relations—which means where you get your local store to participate in its community." In other words, he explained, "giving money to charities is the easiest way to go."

"Community relations" meant that McDonald's was to be found where the action was, where the media wires crossed and emotions ran high. And nowhere was this more so than at the scenes of calamities and at sickbeds. Wherever disease or disaster struck, Mr. McDonald's could be expected to storm in with an armload of free hamburgers.

Mr. McDonald's was in Santa Cruz, California, during the state's worst snowstorm in ten years; in Joplin, Missouri, after it got hit by a tornado; in Roseville, California, after an ammunition train exploded; in Cleveland, Ohio, to lead a "Lead Poisoning Awareness Week"; in Southeast Florida with a "Hospital Coloring Book for Young People"; in San Diego, California, with a Bike-a-Thon for Diabetes; in Saint Petersburg, Florida, when a Goodwill warehouse burned down; in Roanoke, Virginia, at the death of Frump Frump, an elephant in the zoo; in Vietnam, with an assortment of crew hats, hamburger baskets, and Ronald McDonald banks; and nationwide on the Jerry Lewis Labor Day Muscular Dystrophy Telethon, the longest fund-raising marathon in TV history, which featured a special McDonald's tote board showing the money pledges flip over like the numbers on a billion-burger board. Hamburger Central's *Management Newsletter*—fittingly subtitled "Learning the System"—noted that the telethon had been shown over 153 stations and a special spot with Jerry Lewis and Ronald McDonald in McDonaldland was shown on most of them.

But as Mr. McDonald's chased the bandwagon and public attention, there were times when he found himself hoist on his own petard. One such case involved a town in Virginia, which denounced Mr. McDonald's when they learned of the conditions attached to the gift of an elephant to the local zoo. Among the stipulations accompanying the gift were that a permanent plaque be placed on the elephant's living quarters naming the donor; and that the elephant would be named Ronnie McDonald if a female, or Ronald if a male. In the end, the zoo got its elephant from the chairman of a local motel chain, who made a point of stressing angrily that his gift came "with no strings attached."

Mr. McDonald's self-serving community spirit has also drawn opposition from unexpected quarters. A number of communities, offended by his round-the-clock display of the flag, claimed that by law it should not be flown after sunset.

Having installed nighttime illumination at all of its stands, one Mr. McDonald's defended the practice by citing the U.S. Army Institute of Heraldry, the American Legion, the Library of Congress, the U.S. Senate and the Massachusetts state legislature, explaining that the flag was displayed "as part of a program that encourages Americans to build up their country and not tear it down."

When not present at the scenes of calamity or civic events, Mr. McDonald's liked to be seen with celebrities. He was never happier than when he served VIP's, politicians, the stars of sports, stage, and screen. He was positively in his element during *Esquire* magazine's gala 1970 "Salute to the Sixties" at New York's Peppermint Lounge, where the campy crowd, feasting on Big Macs and MacFries, included Otto Preminger, Chubby Checker, Senators George Murphy and Jacob Javits, Mike Nichols, and Katharine Hepburn. Mr. McDonald's was overjoyed when he discovered that the children of Senator Edward Kennedy ate at McDonald's, and he happily obliged by sending a Big Mac by commercial jet to London for a Hollywood actor who appeared to be overcome by hamburger cravings.

The rolling stock of the PR caravan was Hamburger Central's fleet of Big Mac buses, nominally owned by Ray Kroc, which crisscrossed the United States on itineraries charted in the office of Cooper and Golin. Also known as Sunshine coaches, their normal freight consisted of paraplegics, muscular dystrophy victims, orphans, the deaf and dumb, senior citizens, as well as entertainment and sports figures like Bob Griese of the Miami Dolphins and the Johnny Mann Singers, politicians like the city council members of Dubuque, and New York State beauty pageant contestants. Big Mac accommodated Radio City Music Hall bandleader Paul Lavelle, director of McDonald's All-American Marching Band, and a group of Illinois politicians who traveled aboard the hamburger bus to visit a state capital. Prince Philip of the United Kingdom was honored by Al Golin with a special escort of two Sunshine coaches for the prince's favorite charity, Variety Clubs International, a theatrical organization that builds hospitals and sanatoriums for crippled children. One McDonald's employee held a wedding reception aboard Big Mac, and the bus transported Ray Kroc in style to the home opener of his San Diego Padres baseball team.

"We did everything," recalls Al Golin about the early days when he set out to make Mr. McDonald's a star. "Every crazy, nutty thing you could think of, and many of the things we did in those days are still in effect today."

Al Golin took personal charge of Mr. McDonald's more sensational public appearances. In 1965 he overcame the objections of Stock Exchange officials to invade the Exchange floor with free hamburgers on the occasion of McDonald's listing on the board. And when the company sold its first billion hamburgers, Golin marked this milestone by having the world's biggest hamburger cooked and served it in Washington, D.C., to some five hundred people, including Department of Agriculture officials and other notables.

The success of Golin's saturation blitz was evident as early as 1965, when McDonald's was chosen to represent the United States during West Berlin's "Green Week" at a U.S. Information Agency–sponsored trade pavilion designed to promote the sale of American beef in Europe. McDonald's was selected, said a USIA press release, because in the last ten years "the name McDonald's and hamburger have become virtually synonymous."

Two years after receiving its credentials as America's prime hamburger spokesman, McDonald's launched its first national advertising campaign. From the first day it was to match and eventually exceed the intensity of the Cooper and Golin publicity apparatus. In previous years, McDonald's operators had advertised only on a local level, but in 1967 a full-scale coordinated national advertising budget was launched with a whopping $5 million. Two years later the ad budget had grown to nearly $15 million. By 1973 it was $50 million, and a year later it was estimated as a $60 million massive campaign that drowns competitors by sheer, overpowering weight. McDonald's today ranks among the top thirty advertisers in the country.

Time magazine, in its McDonald's cover story, hailed the "burger that conquered the country." But, if America fell, it was to the battle cry that is enscrolled in the office of McDonald's advertising director at Hamburger Central:

> Early to bed
> Early to rise
> Advertise
> Advertise
> Advertise

The effect of the advertising assault was most obvious to hot dog merchants. By 1971 the whole hot-dog industry was in disarray. The Oscar Mayer Company's sales had fallen by 2 percent in one year. The hamburger warriors were advancing on all fronts of the dwindling market. Ray Krock was about to kick the hot dog from the baseball stands, in fact. "They just don't know," moaned Oscar Mayer, Jr. "They just don't know."

The hot dog's position was precarious indeed. Almost half of the people questioned by the Hygrade Food Products Laboratory in Detroit said they were fed up with the frank. Bess Myerson, New York City's former consumer-affairs commissioner, personally advised people not to touch the stuff. *Life* magazine analyzed a hot dog and found it to be mainly fat and water. The current frank, charged *Consumer Reports*, had less protein than the frank of the depression. The wiener, admitted the president of the American Meat Institute, was "being clobbered."

In this dark hour, Oscar Mayer turned to the same weapon that McDonald's had used to such great effect. It launched a barrage of advertising and promotional stunts. It began by giving out blue, red, and white badges saying "Hooray! For the hot dog." It ordered the director of its consumer affairs division to hit sixty-three cities in twelve weeks and spread "the truth about the hot dog." Company spokesmen defended the weiner to newspaper editors and talk-show hosts, while consumers were showered with a countrywide blizzard of pamphlets called "Our Hot Dog Stand." Half of Oscar Mayer's $8 to $10 million TV advertising budget was switched to bolstering the image of the hot dog.

The wiener's counterattack gave courage to others. Packers, producers, and distributors across the country soon joined in. Jordan's Ready-To-Eat Meats in Portland, Maine, ran a full-page newspaper ad: "A Frank Statement about a Lot of Baloney." The wiener's chiefs of staff, the National Hot Dog and Sausage Council, invited a NASA official to lecture 140 food editors on the delights of the hot dog, who told the gathering that the Skylab astronauts favored "the hot dog as an all-American reminder of home." The hot dog, he confidently predicted, "will probably go to Mars someday."

It was an axiom of the trade that the benefits from advertising were in direct proportion to the amount of money spent. Money bought exposure. In a matter of five years, advertising was the principal expenditure of Hamburger Central and with its huge outlay of money, McDonald's managed to overwhelm the smaller chains and survive the franchise "shake-out" that took place in 1970. For instance, it was nothing for Hamburger Central to air five commercials in the space of three hours over a Saint Louis TV station. In 1973 McDonald's $4 million Los Angeles ad budget alone was the biggest in the region.

The cost of this huge national program was borne by many franchised shoulders, with McDonald's operators contributing—*on top of* their regular levies—3 to 4 percent of their annual gross sales. From this constantly growing pool, Hamburger Central maintained a national advertising agency, as well as sixty-three sub agencies throughout the United States.

The latter served local operators who were grouped in advertising co-ops designed to publicize their joint promotional activities.

Because of the number of McDonald's stands, especially in highly populated areas, the advertising clout of the co-ops was tremendous. The ad co-op in the Chicago area could band together 120 operators to sponsor the city's 1973 Christmas Day Parade. Some 150 Ohio stands could chip in $285 apiece for the exclusive sponsorship of Ohio's 1973 State Fair. Above all, the local advertising could be tailored to the national campaign in order to saturate one particular region.

McDonald's first national advertising campaign turned out to be a success that astounded even the top echelons. It ended with a grand finale that saw 10 million children write in to pick the riders on the floats in Macy's Thanksgiving Day Parade in New York. The company's first national TV special was equally successful, featuring James Stewart at the World Boy Scout Jamboree in Idaho, along with McDonald's operators who were hooked into local Boy Scout councils to honor fund-raising cards entitling the donor to a free feast. Other promotional paraphernalia included the usual flood of direct mailings, newspaper ads, bumper stickers, and window posters that became standard for subsequent campaigns. Typical of McDonald's later commercials was "Lonely Mom," which received the 1973 CLIO advertising award as the year's best commercial in the Retail Food/Restaurant category. "Lonely Mom" predictably drowns her sorrows by eating a hamburger at McDonald's.

One of the company's early advertising forays that did not receive any kudos was a $500,000 sweepstakes that ran as an advertising insert in 18.9 million copies of the *Reader's Digest*. The prizes ranged from station wagons to high-intensity lamps, and the ad listed "preselected" numbers that readers were asked to take to their local McDonald's, where winning numbers were posted. But in a subsequent investigation, the Federal Trade Commission charged McDonald's with having misrepresented the offer—that of the 15,610 prizes listed, only 227 were actually awarded, for a total value of $13,000, and that McDonald's had given the ad firm which ran the contest a fee of $25,000, with which it was obliged to pay for all the $500,000 worth of prizes! Ultimately, however, the FTC decided that the promotion of the sweepstakes offer was not deceptive or misleading.

D'Arcy was the advertising agency which originated the early theme that pitched McDonald's as "Your Kind of Place." It clung cautiously to the surburban stereotypes—a child in a McDonald's with the standard sprinkling of freckles and the gap between two incisors. In 1970, however, this image was broadened under the new advertising command of Needham, Harper and Steers, one of the top agencies in the country, (one client was Lassie). Though retaining the basic family orientation, Needham ushered in a program of more sophisticated ads aimed at the parents with the slogan "You Deserve a Break Today" and at their children with the character of Ronald McDonald. The stress no longer would be on food or value. It was the "McDonald's Experience."

An account executive explained what this meant. "The message we're trying to get across is that going to McDonald's can be a fun experience for an American family. For a housewife, it's a mini-break in the day's routine. For Dad it's an opportunity to be a hero to the kids, but in a way which won't cost much money. For the children, it's plain fun. For all of them it's a family-oriented thing."

The McDonald's Experience was to include gaudy packaging that put everything from hamburgers to apple pies inside colorful wrappers and boxes. Also the conversion to customized stores, such as the stand in Hollywood that resembled a theater lobby, complete with an eight-foot sign trimmed, lit, and lettered like an old movie marquee: "Now Playing McDonald's featuring . . . Big Mac." And in the era of adult entertainment came the adult hamburger, the Quarter Pounder, a beefy masculine hulk.

Music was an important part in promoting the grown up

hamburger. According to a Needham executive, it was to inspire a "feeling . . . an urge to get away from what you ordinarily do." This evolved into the seductive theme song created by the same music publishing company that did the Pan Am tune and Kodak's "Make Your Picture Count." "Up, Up and Away" became the close model for it.

McDonald's own confidential "Product Q Study" for 1973, a national survey of fast-food usage among U.S. families, apparently recognized the success of the combination hoopla and hamburger by noting that McDonald's image on quality, cleanliness, value and service had remained static—while overall the company continued to expand its share of the market. These results indicated that people appeared to be seeking something more than a hamburger and french fries. Customers actually did visit McDonald's for a break from routine.

Not surprisingly, the McDonald's Experience fixed its most intense focus on children, the path of least resistance to the consumer purse. Children took their cues almost entirely from TV. They were "surrogate salesmen," in the words of author Vance Packard, and the crudest advertising was directed at them. Hamburger Central's own data has been quoted as showing that in three out of four families, children decided where to eat. So, with this in mind, the Needham ad firm created the strange fantasy world called McDonaldland where consumption was the primary activity of its bizarre inhabitants. Big Mac, the chief of patty police, drove around in a black paddy wagon and tended the security system which includes a Burger Alarm and a large policeman's whistle. City Hall was occupied by Mayor McCheese, a close ally of Big Mac, who had gained office by promising "honesty and goodness to all." Mayor McCheese professed dedication to solving the problems of McDonaldland as crime appeared to be rampant. Thieves, fast-food addicts and burger muggers made life unsafe in the Hamburger Patch, among the Apple Pie Trees. Big Mac was constantly blowing his whistle, while the wail of the Burger Alarm kept McDonaldland in the grip of fear.

Chief among Big Mac's targets was the Hamburglar who
inevitably ended up being taken away in the paddy wagon.
There was Evil Grimace, a purple blob, enslaved to McDonald's shakes, who answered almost every question with "GEE,
I'M THIRSTY!" And then there was Captain Crook, the Filet-O-
Fish pirate. But the top authority of the law-and-order regime
was Ronald McDonald, the clown prince of McDonaldland.

Ronald McDonald's permanent home is in Hollywood, on
the world's largest children's commercial stage set. According
to the *San Diego Union,* the stage shows the Hamburger
Patch with its talking buns, the Apple Pie Trees, and all
the other McDonaldland accouterments. The various regional
districts each have similar sets for their own McDonaldland
promotions. It was the set borrowed from the mid-Atlantic
Region, for instance, that graced the Ohio State Fair, a show
that featured the defeat of the Hamburglar and Captain Crook
in their attempts to turn McDonaldland into Messyland.

The McDonaldland set in Hollywood seems to show the
influence of Disney's realm in nearby Anaheim. The commercials similarly have the touch of the Sherman brothers,
Richard and Robert, who worked on such Disney films as *Mary
Poppins* and on the *Reader's Digest*–produced *Tom Sawyer.*
The McDonaldland set was designed by Don Ament, a former
art director for Columbia Pictures and Screen Gems, and in
recent years Ament's Setmaker, Inc. has been busy supplying
and creating the special designs for the McDonaldland Parks
that are rapidly springing up in different parts of the country.

The first McDonaldland Park, complete with a Golden
Arch–shaped bridge, was built in 1973 in Chula Vista, California, just five miles north of the Mexican border. Closely
modeled on the Hollywood stage set, its opening was attended
by the children of prominent civic, military, and business
leaders. The high point of the ceremony, according to news
accounts, was the snipping of a string of dollar bills, super-
vised by McDonald's publicist, Chuck Buck. The children,
wearing McDonald's "VIP" hats, were served hamburgers and

"kiddie cocktails" as they wandered through the Hamburger Patch and the grove of Apple Pie Trees, or relaxed by the Filet-O-Fish Fountain and inspected the statuary.

For live local appearances, Hamburger Central maintains some fifty Ronald McDonalds on its payroll throughout the country. These are in turn divided into "greeting" and "performing" clowns. Anyone playing the clown is required by McDonald's to attend regular seminars so as to maintain a uniform image. A special "Ronald trainer" was even hired to travel around the country to make sure the buffoons conformed.

Ronald McDonald's growing stature in the company was underscored by a recent Ronald McDonald convention of clowns. With his promotional image translated in a subsidiary hamburger industry, Oak Brook urged its franchisees to buy Ronald wristwatches, or a fifty-five-dollar electric wall clock with Ronald McDonald swinging to and fro as a pendulum. Thus Ronald McDonald and his cohorts were incorporated into Hamburger Central's growing list of premium items as Ronald McDonald and Hamburglar dolls, as well as a "McDonald's at home" toy stand by Playskool that included a building and 19 accessory pieces. A live Ronald McDonald could even be had as part of a McDonald's birthday package at the store where the clown did simple magic tricks, tied balloons, and told jokes.

The examples of Ronald McDonald and the other denizens of the Hamburger Patch have been slavishly followed by McDonald's competitors. And as in the case of the hot dog, the battle was fought with advertising. Burger Chef added the "funburger," a hamburger that came with a toy in a box, and Burger King came out with a Burger King doll shortly after the Ronald McDonald doll made its appearance. Burger King also launched an ad assault aimed at children with "Where Kids Are King," complete with free paper crowns; and at adults with the slogan "It takes two hands to handle a Whopper," which showed such sports personalities as Wilt

Chamberlain and Sam Snead wrap their grip around a mound of ground beef.

With over one thousand stands and backed by the giant Pillsbury Corporation, Burger King remained McDonald's closest rival in the mass-retailing of hamburgers. Oak Brook's intelligence operations regarding Burger King's activities were thought to be especially thorough. The results of the closely guarded "Product Q Study" noted that, of the major national chains, Burger King had shown the strongest growth in family patronage since 1972. But still more alarming was the news of Burger King's plans to spend $3 million between October and December on a fresh ad offensive. The campaign would be aimed at McDonald's "uncustomized," assembly-line hamburger. TV spots would depict a Burger King as the "one place you can get exactly what you want." The Burger King campaign evolved into the rousing "Have It Your Way" theme song.

But the most successful challenge of Ronald McDonald's hamburger hegemony did not come from the Whopper. It came from a cute little five-year-old black salesman from Long Beach, California. His name was Rodney Allen Rippee, and his meteoric rise to stardom came as the singer of a bouncy commercial for Jack in the Box, which featured Jumbo Jack, Big Mac's jaw-busting rival. "Make Life a Little Easier," Rodney Rippee crooned in an engaging falsetto, rolling his big eyes and laughing as his cheeks dimpled.

Rodney Rippee came out of the office of Doyle Dane Bernbach, the creators of the Dreyfus lion and the famed Volkswagen and the "We Try Harder" Avis ads. A poll taken after his first TV appearances revealed that 90 percent of the people who saw the commercials remembered the child star, and a whopping 89 percent remembered that he was selling hamburgers for Jack in the Box. According to a Doyle executive, this was the "highest awareness reading" in a business where a 40 percent awareness of an advertisement is generally considered "phenomenal."

Rodney Rippee's overnight success spread from California to national exposure on talk shows, TV specials, and films. Big Mac was up against Jumbo Jack. There were also attacks from other fronts. The Bonanza International chain of steak houses put up outdoor advertising with the bold copy "You Deserve a Steak Today"; as well as "Try Our T-Bone, It's BIG, MAC." Der Wienerschnitzel, a West Coast hot dog chain, went one better when it urged the public to take "a break from the hamburger habit."

Amid the high-sloganeering passions of the Patty War, McDonald's moved forward its heaviest weapon, the Quarter Pounder, the Big Bertha of the burger arsenal. Like a long-awaited super-weapon, it was rolled out in 1972 and paraded before the Investment Analysts Society of Chicago, at McDonald's Honolulu convention, and at McDonald's annual stockholders meeting in Oak Brook. It was to replace the "double" hamburger, which then sold for forty cents. The new Quarter Pounder went on the market for fifty-three cents.

Figures showed that the average McDonald's customer came in fewer than two times a month—and only 10 percent of the residents surrounding each McDonald's came in more than once a month. As a result, the new promotional effort was to be directed at gaining more "repeats." Advertising for the Quarter Pounder was increased.

In the beginning, it scored notable successes. Its heavy stress on value came at a time when inflation began eating markedly into the consumer's pocket, and sales of the Quarter Pounder were an important element in McDonald's subsequent rise in quarterly profits. "The Quarter Pounder," Fred Turner cheerfully announced to the shareholders, "is one of the most successful of all our menu additions."

But as profits rolled up, a letter arrived at the Federal Trade Commission asking for an investigation of McDonald's superburger. The letter had been sent by Democratic Congressman Benjamin Rosenthal of New York, and it requested the im-

mediate issuance of a cease and desist order against all
McDonald's advertising relating to the Quarter Pounder.

At Rosenthal's request, the U.S. Department of Agriculture
had run a series of tests on Quarter Pounders purchased from
a number of different McDonald's outlets. Rosenthal informed
the FTC that in no instance had the grilled beef in the Quarter
Pounder weighed more than three ounces—a full ounce less
than promised in McDonald's multimillion-dollar ad campaign! "In fact," said the congressman, "the amount of beef by
weight in the Quarter Pounders averages between 2½ and 2¾
ounces." He charged that the typical ads falsely offered a
"quarter-pound 100% beef patty."

The New York representative compared a Quarter Pounder
—which weighed 2 4/7 ounces—with two of McDonald's
regular hamburgers, which together contained 2 1/4 ounces:
that is, only 1/4 ounce less than the Quarter Pounder. "But,"
explained Rosenthal, "the Quarter Pounder costs fifty-three
cents to the two hamburgers at forty cents, and the two hamburgers have twice as much roll."

Rosenthal cited the USDA tests as showing that McDonald's
Double Hamburger offered consumers much better value than
the more expensive Quarter Pounder. He charged that Mc-
Donald's had deliberately dropped the Double Hamburger
and Cheeseburger from its menu "to avoid comparisons embarrassing to the company." Rosenthal asked the FTC to in-
vestigate under the "unfair trade practices" statutes of the
Federal Trade Commission Act. "Many product brand names
are inherently deceptive to the consumer," he wrote, "and it is
up to the FTC to take action against them."

Rosenthal's letter cited the Quarter Pounder as an example
of "hidden inflation." McDonald's substitution of a lower-value
product at a comparatively higher price further cheapened the
food dollar, the congressman said. However, the FTC did not
find it so. While Congressman Rosenthal bristled with new
charges that the FTC had abandoned its "'get-tough' policy
on false and misleading advertising," Hamburger Central re-

sponded quickly. In September, 1973, it ordered all Quarter Pounder advertising to be reviewed by McDonald's Legal Department and directed that all Big Mac and Quarter Pounder commercials be temporarily replaced with non-meat commercials.

Hamburger Central published a list of procedures to follow when an official of the Bureau of Weights and Measures appeared on the McDonald's premises. The store manager was instructed to examine the official's badge and identification card and to write down his name and number. He was told to be present during the entire test and to make certain the scale was placed on a flat surface and that there were no drafts across the weighing area. Advertisements later emphasized the point that the Quarter Pounder was a quarter of a pound *before* cooking.

The Colonel's Story

"I Used to Cuss the Prettiest You Ever Heard"

A couple of years ago Ray Kroc ran into Colonel Sanders outside the Century Plaza Hotel in Los Angeles. The Colonel looked overweight and troubled, Kroc says, but he still swore like a trooper. Ray Kroc had the greatest respect for Harland Sanders. But back in 1964, the Colonel had made the mistake of selling out his finger lickin' recipe for a measly sum that also tied him to a contract as a roving ambassador for Kentucky Fried Chicken.

"That friggin' bootline outfit," Kroc recalls the Colonel sputtering, while leaning on his hand-carved walking cane. "They prostituted every goddamn thing I had. I had the greatest gravy in the world and those sons of bitches, they dragged it out and extended it and watered it down that I'm so goddamn mad." Kroc remembers the Colonel as saying.

The Colonel was wearing his customary white linen suit and black string tie with diamond pin. His goatee and whiskers were white as snow: he looked exactly as he did on the big candy-striped buckets that revolved in the sky over four thousand chicken stands around the world—but when the Colonel got so goddamn mad his cheeks flushed and his goatee quivered.

Harland Sanders' early career had been harsher than Ray Kroc's. Born in 1890, he was raised on a poor Indiana farm. In the fifth grade he had been forced to quit school. He labored on farms, soldiered in Cuba, and tried his hand at a grabbag of trades. He had been employed as a streetcar conductor, fireman, and ferryboat pilot; he had studied law by correspondence; he had sold insurance and tires; he had worked as secretary of the Columbus, Indiana, Chamber of Commerce; he had manufactured acetylene lighting systems; he had operated a service station, and finally, in the little Kentucky hilltown of Corbin, he had opened a restaurant that quickly gained fame for its pan-fried chicken, stringbeans, ham, okra, biscuits, fresh salads. And it was there, after years of experimenting in his cramped country kitchen, that he developed his secret blend of eleven herbs and spices.

The Hamburger King and the Colonel liked each other. They shared the kinship of the open road. They knew the length and breadth of this road and the dreams built alongside it.

"How come you're still making commercials?" the Hamburger King asked Sanders.

"What the hell," Kroc recalls the Colonel saying bitterly, shaking his white head. "They gave me a dirty deal and it's the only way I get any money. I have to make commercials. I didn't get enough in the first place. Obviously I have to smile and my face is on the picture, so at least I get that benefit."

Some years earlier Kroc says the Colonel had privately warned him that if McDonald's ever broke into chicken it would create "chaos." Hamburger Central's interest in chicken dated back to 1968, when it first began tests. It continued testing chicken in 1970. But a year later the pullet-to-patron process was still hopelessly snagged. The problem was working the bugs out of the special fryers and setting up a mass-distribution network that could deliver a consistent, juicy chicken. By the first quarter of 1974 only one McDonald's stand in Virginia was selling chicken on a trial basis. McDonald's was still a long way away from doing to the pullet what it had done to the patty, and Kroc and the Colonel were still the best of friends.

The winter following their accidental meeting, Kroc says he heard from his friend again. The Hamburger King was staying at his Fort Lauderdale home. The Colonel called from a hospital in North Carolina that specialized in a rice diet for high blood pressure and weight reduction.

"What the hell are you doing up there?" Kroc remembers barking over the phone. "*You* want to reduce. You're eighty years old."

The Colonel sounded tired to Kroc. He said he was eighty-two and had eighteen more years to go before he had to retire himself.

In the thirties, Harland Sanders had been made an honorary colonel in the Kentucky Guard. Governor Ruby Laffoon, who conferred the rank, did so in recognition of Sanders' contribution to the state cuisine; the fame of Sanders' Corbin restaurant had spread up and down the Southern highways, far enough to be singled out for praise in Duncan Hines's 1939 *Adventures in Good Eating*.

It was also in 1939 that the Colonel made a breakthrough that would revolutionize the chicken industry. It had to do with the cooking of the chicken.

In recent years, food engineers have explained the phenomenon of "chicken fatigue," the fact that people get tired sooner of eating chicken than beef. They say this is because the flavor from any cut of beef comes from the tiny flecks of fat lacing the meat, and that these are distributed in such a way that the better-tasting, more expensive cuts of meat are those with the optimum amount of fat. In chicken, however, the fat is contained entirely within the skin or just beneath it, resulting in dull-tasting meat.

But in his bustling Corbin restaurant the Colonel found a way of maintaining the chicken's flavor, preserving its moisture, and soft texture, and doing it all in a mere eight or nine minutes. His previous pan-frying method had taken as long as thirty minutes. French-frying the chicken in a wire basket in deep fat had proved faster, but it produced a chicken that was dry, crusty, and unevenly done.

The Colonel then turned to a relatively new utensil, the pressure cooker. And after months of experimentation, he managed to cook up a chicken that pleased him.

The career of Harland Sanders had been a series of ups and downs. Like Ray Kroc, he had never been one to let opportunity slip by unheeded, but each time the vision of success had gone aglimmer. In 1941 he opened another restaurant in the small town of Berea, sixty-five miles north of Corbin. Business was good, and he decided to build Kentucky's first motel. But in the early fifties the new Interstate 75 was built to bypass his roadside establishments, killing his trade.

Forced to liquidate, Colonel Sanders at age sixty-six possessed a small amount of cash, a monthly Social Security check for $105, and an unbounded faith in his secret method for flavoring and cooking chicken. Ray Kroc had already spent a year selling hamburger franchises when he was joined on the road by Colonel Harland Sanders, older by a dozen years, who set out to do the same for his special-recipe, pressure-cooked chicken.

While Kroc and Sanders, respectively, traveled the United States, they could see the grid of highways changing. By the mid-fifties, a huge $76 billion federal interstate highway building program had been launched to further stimulate the interdependence between the automobile and roadside franchising. As the Colonel negotiated this growing network, he sat upright in his antiquated car. Whenever he spotted a likely-looking restaurant he stopped, unloaded his pressure cooker and bag of secret seasoning and asked the owner to let him cook some chicken. Flogging his franchises from door to door, often accompanied by the "Colonel's lady"—his wife, Claudia—Harland Sanders demonstrated his recipe, awed the cooks, and sold the license for a four cent royalty per serving.

It was a painstakingly slow and primitive method. The Colonel did his own bookkeeping and paperwork, while his lady took care of the mixing, packing, and shipping of the secret formula. By 1960 his tireless travels had yielded some four hundred menu-item franchises in the United States and about a half dozen in Canada.

But even more pervasive than the fame of his recipe was the spread of his name as a minor celebrity. Wherever he went in his white suit and string tie, people stopped and stared. He looked like a character from a story book, redolent of mint julep and magnolia. People took to the kindly-looking gentleman and over the years the product and the Colonel merged into a human trademark. What people didn't know was the awful language the kindly-looking trademark could utter. "I used to cuss the prettiest you ever heard," the Colonel reminisced in a *New Yorker* profile several years ago.

His father had died when he was six and he had grown up under the strict discipline of his mother. Respectful of her strictures, he would never during all his life smoke, drink, or play cards. But his language apparently flowered to the point where he would pray for the Lord to help him swear off the cursed habit of cussing in front of women or anybody else.

This compulsion to cuss did not interfere with the success of his franchise business and, as a growing number of menus multiplied his name, he probably cussed less. In 1960 he could afford to give up travel, since his fame had reached the point where prospective franchisees gladly traveled to see him. The select among them returned home not with his recipe but a license. The Colonel kept the recipe for the secret gravy securely under lock and key. No one, except the colonel's lady,

was entrusted with it. The Colonel guarded the formula zealously, because, unlike the Hamburger King, he considered
himself more than a salesman and a promoter.

While his mother worked in a nearby canning factory, Harland Sanders began cooking at age six for his younger brother
and sister. His love of the culinary art was genuine. At advanced age his lack of formal education did not prevent him
from attending Cornell's School of Hotel and Restaurant Administration, as well as undertaking similar studies at the
University of Chicago. Among his friends, he was famous for
his sourdough pancakes, barbecued ribs, stews, chili, bread,
oyster soup and desserts of all kinds. But to Sanders himself
the supreme stuff of his art was his gravy, the blend of herbs
and spices that time and patience had taught him. It was his
ambition to make a gravy so good that people would simply
eat the gravy and throw away "the durned chicken."

But the greatest gravy in the world, the sauce that would
make masses of people delirious, never came to pass. In 1964
Harland Sanders sold out to two Nashville businessmen, a
lawyer and a financier. The Colonel's gravy was fantastic, they
agreed, according to an article in *Business Week*, but it was
too complex, too time-consuming, too expensive. It had to be
changed. It wasn't fast food.

The two men had apparently spent months wooing and
coaxing. The two were the financier Jack C. Massey, the former
owner of a surgical supply house, and a young, tall, and hand-
some lawyer, John Y. Brown, Jr., then twenty-nine, about half
Massey's age.

As a boy, John Brown, Jr., is said to have been a sales
prodigy, a virtuoso of the door-to-door spiel; at sixteen, he was
pulling in $700 a month selling vacuum cleaners; as a freshman
at the University of Kentucky he turned to selling encyclo-
pedias, clearing as much as $500 a weekend. He became a
multimillionaire at age thirty-one, two years after buying out
Kentucky Fried Chicken.

As principal stockholders, Massey became chairman and

Brown president of a loosely knit chain of six hundred outlets
that it had taken the Colonel ten years to develop. KFC's subsequent expansion was the most phenomenal in the fast-food
field, outstripping even McDonald's. By 1970 its sales were
approaching $1 billion. With nearly 6,000 units in some forty
countries, serving almost two million chickens a day, it now
ranks as the largest food retail operation in the world.

John Brown, Jr., had changed the franchise concept from
walk-up stores and restaurant menu items to a strictly take-
home operation. The design of the chicken shops was homogenized into the standard red-and-white-striped buildings.
Under Brown, the Colonel's operation was put on a streamlined footing. Managers and franchisees were trained at Kentucky Fried Chicken University in Louisville and an engineering director, Art Pelster, was hired from the aircraft industry
to experiment with shortening and to solve the problem of
maintaining uniform quality in the seasoning and flour. The
company claimed it had located the most uniform flour in the
world in regions of Illinois and Texas and engineer Pelster
continued to work on a combination breading machine and
cooker that would be the next-best thing to having the
Colonel himself. This setup quickly produced profits and
speculators. A $5,000 investment in KFC stock in 1964 was
worth $3.5 million five years later.

The oldest franchisees, with as many as thirty or forty of the
Colonel's stands, formed corporations of their own. One of
these was Pete Harmon, Harland Sanders' first franchisee,
whom he had met while attending the food-service school at
the University of Chicago in the early fifties. Harmon acquired
the KFC territory for Utah and much of the West and in '64
joined Brown and Massey in buying out the Colonel, becoming
a vice-president and director of the new corporation.

The Colonel's recipe subsequently cooked up millions of
dollars for well over 125 other franchisees and corporate
employees—all of it in a few short years. Ironically, the person

who apparently made the least out of his recipe was the Colonel himself. He had been outfoxed and plucked like one of his own chickens by more able businessmen.

Along with the $2 million in cash, Sanders had kept the KFC franchises in Canada. Having to spend part of the year away from home in Shelbyville, Kentucky, he bought a house in Toronto, Ontario, and, along with his other travels, he became a globe-trotting exile for part of the year.

Even though Brown and Massey had altered his gravy to the point where the Colonel would sputter that it was "slop" that should be served with a straw, the corporation insisted on its "secret" composition and, in order to minimize the number of people sharing this "secret," franchisees were not allowed to know the recipe either. They were required to buy the patented blend of herbs and spices from the company. "Only Sanders, Massey, and the company's food engineer know the recipe," *Business Week* reported reverently in 1967.

The "secret," "special," or "miracle" ingredient is engrained in the lore of the fast-food giants. At the Jack in the Box Food Maker plant in Kearny Mesa, California, the chief of public relations maintained with a straight face that its own secret sauce was known to only one man in the organization—"some little Mexican cook in the plant."

McDonald's boasts its own mayonnaise-based Secret Sauce—"the formula of which," *Time* magazine wrote, "is guarded like an atomic secret." But the real basis of the secret sauce was far less mysterious, according to Ray Kroc: "Every franchise in the entire United States sells products to their operators, and they've been hauled back and forth into court. Like Kentucky Fried Chicken licensees claimed that they were paying three to four to five times for the same herbs and for the same chicken, and that they could get it from Durkee's or Kraft or any big company in the United States. And Kentucky Fried Chicken said, no, you couldn't because the formula was a secret.

"You know that was a lot of crap. Any laboratory can tell you what's in it. There's no platinum in there. There's no gold in there. So how the hell are you going to get the price?"

When Brown and Massey made their deal with Colonel Sanders, they received title to all the Sanders patents and trademarks, including the Colonel's "image"; the slogan "It's finger lickin' good"; and the term "Tender and Tasty Colonel Sanders Kentucky Fried Chicken." From the standpoint of the new owners, the image must have been the crucial part of the agreement. They evidently realized that Sanders had been selling the wrong thing all along. The Colonel had been promoting his gravy—when he should have been promoting himself.

"He's the greatest PR man I have ever known," Massey would marvel later. Nevertheless, one of the first things John Brown, Jr., did as president of the new company was to hire another PR man in New York, whence Harland Sanders began his worldwide trek of a quarter million miles a year; a circuit as regular as clockwork that saw him popping up each year on the same TV shows, parades, festivals, charities, awards, store-openings. He ventured out in fair weather and foul, refusing to wear a coat over his famous white suit.

His visit to Tokyo created a minor sensation. In New Mexico, Navajos jingled, "America loves what the Colonel cooks." The Colonel appeared in small cameo roles in a couple of movies. A Hollywood producer announced plans to make a feature film of his life and Harland Sanders sat down to work on his autobiography, *Finger Lickin' Good*.

No one had better understood the full promotional possibilities of the Colonel than John Y. Brown, Jr. He skillfully built the product around the image, from the store-front sign of the Colonel's face to its multiple reproduction on cartons, buckets, and a flood of big-budget advertising. Testifying in January, 1970, before the Senate Small Business Select Committee, John

Brown, Jr., paid tribute to the "image"—a human trademark which, unlike Aunt Jemima or Betty Crocker, could walk, talk, and sell.

"Colonel Sanders founded the company," he told the senators. "He sells the southern flavor and the southern sizzle of the southern product." A year later Brown and Massey sold Kentucky Fried Chicken, and with it the Colonel. "We just plain grew too fast," Brown was quoted as saying, as KFC stock plummeted and profits slid downhill in the late sixties.

KISS—Keep It Simple, Stupid—the Colonel's basic principle had been ignored. KFC had begun to manufacture a range of items, from mint candy to barbecue sauce, put the chicken in the motel business, diversified into roast beef and fish and chips, and each year brought out more and more franchises with the massively inflated pieces of paper stock.

The subsequent strain was too much for one human trademark to bear and, in the South, a new Extra Crispy Chicken had begun to eat into the finger lickin' gravy. So in the spring of 1971 Kentucky Fried Chicken became a subsidiary of Heublein, an aggressive liquor and food conglomerate, which owned Hamm's Beer and a line of condiments, including A-1 Sauce.

Heublein was said to have paid $267 million for the world's biggest chicken chain, and for Brown and Massey the Colonel's gravy proved rich indeed.

Under Massey and Brown, the Colonel had apparently never stopped complaining about the "dirty deal" he'd gotten, and he continued to do so under his new owner, Heublein. For his ambassadorial chores he received $40,000 a year and picked up another $250,000 doing the commercials. He was a millionaire but he belonged to the corporation body and soul, goatee, string tie, and flowing white mane. And he was cussing worse than ever.

Things came to a head in January, 1974, when Sanders filed a $122 million suit against Heublein. "There is no question that the Colonel sold his business and trademarks in 1964," a company spokesman replied, acknowledging that the KFC founder "hasn't been happy about it ever since."

Harland Sanders accused Heublein of trying to interfere with his plans to develop a new franchise operation. Deprived of the title to his own name, he had long operated a restaurant in his hometown of Shelbyville. It was known as "Claudia Sanders, the Colonel's Lady Dinner House," and it featured four entrees—steak, roast beef, ham, and lobster tails. Harland Sanders accused Heublein of threatening his lady's potential franchisees by claiming it would sue her if the Colonel's "image" was used.*

At eighty-four years of age, he geared up for battle. He stressed that the money did not concern him. Neither did he dispute Heublein's legal claim to his image and trademarks. The Colonel simply said that he was obliged to protect his lady. "When anybody does anything to my family, they'll have a fight on their hands."

---

* The Colonel's suit and Heublein's counter suit were both later dropped.

9

Franchise Fever

"Welcome, You Unhappy People!"

On a chilly February morning in 1961 a somber crowd is reported to have gathered before the gates of the New York Coliseum. The line was filled with people from all walks of American life: a dapperly dressed bank clerk; a stooped Alabama chicken farmer; a retired bus driver from upstate New York troubled by medical bills; a Korean War veteran with a disability pension; a middle-aged department store saleslady whose deceased husband had left her an insurance policy; a young bookkeeper's assistant who had saved up $6,000; a schoolteacher who was tired of teaching; a cabdriver tense from battling traffic; a gardener racked by arthritis; a chemical worker with a bad cough; the owner of a failing hardware store in Vermont. The doors opened.

Walking through the gate into the expanse of the Coliseum, they ascended to a large cavernous room where they waited. The future must have looked a little brighter.

They had apparently come to seek guidance and strength,

to beat the time clock and a paycheck that never stretched far enough. Their ideal must have been the small businessman, the independent merchant, the successful member of the community who was hardworking, forthright, and financially sound. And shortly, a leader appeared before them.

His name was A. L. Tunick, a former scrap dealer, the first president of the International Franchise Association, and the lead-off speaker for the Coliseum's much-heralded "Start Your Own Business Exposition."

Tunick had begun franchising Chicken Delight stands in 1952, reportedly after finding a raft of pressure cookers in a factory warehouse about to be demolished for scrap. The cookers had a flaw in them which had led to the factory's bankruptcy, but they could be easily fixed to cook chicken. And within a few years he had an operation in Rock Island, Illinois, that included his own office building, a training school, and the most important structure in the complex—a warehouse from which he shipped all the supplies franchisees were contractually required to buy, just about everything but the chicken. The phenomenal markup on this "tie-in" trade made Tunick a millionaire and a zealous spokesman for the franchise gospel. The more franchises he sold, the more business his warehouse did. Eventually there were hundreds of Chicken Delight stands in nearly every state, including Hawaii, Puerto Rico and Canada.

"*Welcome, you unhappy people!*" Tunick is reported to have barked. "You're here because you are unhappy over your economic lot, your job and your future. Maybe you are happy, but you want to be happier.

"Are you working for $20,000 a year but want to make an easy $50,000 a year? We don't have that for you. Are you making maybe $60, $80, $100 a week, and you'd like to make about $10,000, $15,000 or $20,000 a year, and you are prepared to work hard for it, at least in the initial years?"

"*We have lots of opportunities for you!*"

He is said to have continued narrating the miracle that had rewarded thousands of other Americans.

"True," Tunick reportedly ended, "you must be on solid financial ground to begin with. But if you make up for lack of financial assets with drive and stamina, and if you are *hungry* enough . . . we'll help you get started."

Historically, franchising had always been a way of achieving freedom and independence. The term *franchise* came from the old French word *francher*, meaning "to free," as in freedom from servitude or restraint. During the Middle Ages the Catholic Church would grant "franchises" to friendly personages who served as tax collectors, taking a sizable cut for themselves and remitting the rest to the Pope.

As a method for distributing merchandise, franchising made its appearance in the United States just after the Civil War, when the Singer Sewing Machine Company established a corps of loyal dealers who would soon be found in the world's most remote spots, from the plateaus of the Andes to the steamy banks of the Nile. But the institutionalization of franchising in American life did not occur until 1898, when fledgling General Motors decided to distribute the first steamers through a network of licensed dealers. During the following decade virtually every type of distribution device was experimented with to deliver the automobile to distant markets. The Detroit auto makers sold their vehicles through the mail and some employed traveling salesmen. The horseless carriage was even sold in large department stores.

The first franchisers were production men: auto makers, soft-drink manufacturers, brewers, oil people. Franchising solved the crux of their distribution problem. The franchisor obtained both a source of capital *and* a highly motivated salesman, benefits the Detroit auto makers were among the first to discover from this arrangement. Early on, General Motors had noticed that branch managers just did not display the same degree of motivation to increase sales as the franchisee, who had both his income and business investment to lose.

By granting a franchise to a highly charged businessman, the auto makers saved vast sums of capital. In 1955 *Business Week* estimated that automobile dealer franchises had $4 billion invested in land, buildings, equipment, and inventory. The National Automobile Dealers Association reported that the total investment by these franchised dealers exceeded the total capital invested by all car manufacturers *combined.* In 1968 nearly 95 percent of all U.S. passenger car sales were made by franchisees whose personal investments virtually freed the manufacturers' money for more profitable purposes. In 1970, testifying before Senate Small Business hearings, John Brown, Jr., of Kentucky Fried Chicken estimated that it would take $400 million to build the thousands of franchised stores the company then had in operation.

The system prevailed in the soft-drink and petroleum industry as well, and virtually every beverage company today —including Coca-Cola, Pepsi-Cola and Seven-Up—still follows the same pattern that established the franchised bottler at the turn of the century as the beverage distributor. Coca-Cola currently has thirty-six company-owned plants around the world that produce and sell the syrup and concentrate to some 1,800 bottlers. To get its concoction to consumers, Coca-Cola in the beginning practically gave its licenses away, but today the franchise for a bottling plant requires astronomical sums. A Pepsi-Cola franchise recently sold for $7.6 million, and the bottling plant even became a matter of national diplomacy when President Nixon traveled to Moscow in 1972 with a party that included the chief of Pepsi-Cola, which obtained the Russian territory, while Coca-Cola took the Eastern European market as part of the so-called U.S.-Soviet détente.

The depression saw a franchising spurt on the retail level. The possibilities were demonstrated in the thirties by the sale of cheap, mass-produced fashions in small towns. This came into being when two Lebanese tailors from Los Angeles were unable to find any outlets for their goods. After consigning their first garments to a Glendale, California, store, they decided to sell their low-priced frocks as a franchise under the name Mode O' Day, thereby establishing a chain that would become known in rural America as "the biggest little store in the world." At the same time, door-to-door salespeople took Avon cosmetics and Fuller Brush household wares into virtually every community. An even humbler commodity—softened water—was franchised in 1938 by another small-town entrepreneur in Illinois, who inspired the cry still heard today in hundreds of town and cities throughout the United States— "Oh, Culligan man!"

The real boom in franchising, however, did not come until after the Korean War. Ninety percent of the current 1,200 franchise companies were not in existence before 1954, and the post–World War II shape of American life could be traced along the contours by which franchising took goods to the market. "Business franchises," remarked the prestigious *Management Letter* in 1959, "are growing so rapidly that they're changing basic distribution patterns in a large number of lines." And franchising was never confined to the small business stratum—being rapidly adopted by such giant corporations as B. F. Goodrich; Sears, Roebuck; Swift & Co.; Winchester-Western Division; and Montgomery Ward. *Newsweek* made note that a number of corporate giants were "ironically going to the small businessman for help in reaching new markets."

The franchise fever and the big business boom that occurred simultaneously during the fifties and sixties were closely intertwined. The former came as a reaction to the latter. While the giant corporations enjoyed an unprecedented period of monopolistic growth, the small businessman found himself trapped. He looked for a way to turn, and found the franchise. Billed as the "last frontier of the independent businessman," it lured a stampede of people willing to invest everything to succeed at a time when most small businesses seemed doomed to failure. Invariably, the franchise salesman's most telling pitch was his revelation that nine out of ten nonfranchised businesses failed, whereas for franchised establishments, he would claim, the figure was reversed. Nine out of ten *succeeded*.

Only in those early days of franchising could an aspiring entrepreneur come to a company like McDonald's and utilize the management techniques of a big corporation. For his investment and royalty payments, the "licensee," as Kroc called him, bought the right to share in mass purchasing discounts, making the fifteen-cent hamburger into an economic miracle. For the franchise fee, the company provided a beefy national advertising campaign as well as a constant stream of advice, explaining everything from how to adjust the potato-peeler belt to reports on the energy crisis.

In 1967 the franchise industry recorded sales of about $90 billion, roughly 10 percent of the Gross National Product and 25 percent of the entire retail industry. Excluding gasoline, auto, and the soft-drink industries, the small-business glamour franchisees totaled sales of $13.1 billion, an increase from 1963, when records were started, of 64 percent! And of all the small business franchises for sale, the quick-service, limited-menu chains proved the most dazzling.

The Mom and Pop store, roadside stand, and neighborhood parlor had traditionally been for people who dreamed of establishing business independence. The field had always held out hope for the person who wished to be his own boss, and in post–World War II America it was still largely untapped. In the case of the humble ice-cream stand, for instance, there were only one hundred outlets that served artificial white soft ice cream at the close of World War II. But by 1969 "Softie" or "Frostie Freeze" alone could be bought at any one of 2,600 franchised stands. In 1945 the United States had only 3,500 fast-food outlets altogether; in 1971 there were well over 350,000; in 1975, 440,000.

Two of the oldest and best-known fast-food trademarks

were established in the early twenties at the dawn of the automobile age. In 1922, a Mr. A. (Roy Allen) and a Mr. W. (Fred
Wright) combined forces to start their first A & W root-beer
outlet; and for decades thereafter they continued selling franchises for as little as $50, with the only obligation of the fran-
chisee being the purchase of root-beer concentrate. Another
familiar name was that of Howard Johnson; started in 1925,
it became the chief forerunner of the mass-market menu that
took shape in earnest in 1950 with the establishment of
Dunkin' Donut's first shop. But fast food's big leap forward did
not occur until five years later as Harland Sanders and Ray
Kroc almost simultaneously hit the road to sell their licenses at
a peculiar historical moment.

Franchising flourished during the cold war, and the initial
excitement it created took place not in America's big industrial
metropolises but in the small towns and suburbs. The cold war
and the small town gave franchising a heavily patriotic cast.
Franchising was hailed as an example of capitalism's great
strength over communism. Small-town newspapers especially
played up the theme of the superiority of the free-enterprise
system, using McDonald's as example of the rewards that
could be had by the American individualist who spurned the
collective.

The papers pitted the hamburger business against the Rus-
sians. Pointing out that many of the nation's new entrepreneurs
were getting into business by joining up with drive-in franchises like McDonald's, Pennsylvania's Allentown *Call-Chron-
icle* taunted, "Don't look now, Mr. Khrushchev, but the ranks
of American capitalism are growing by leaps and bounds." In
Florida the Tampa *Tribune* headlined "Franchising Chains
make Capitalists out of Many Folk." A similar headline appeared in the Hartford, Connecticut, *Courant,* "New Capitalists are found in Motel, Drive-In Industry." And it quoted Ray
Kroc: "The franchised drive-in unit is the answer to an
American dream. . . . We're teaching people how to become
successful small businessmen."

Ray Kroc's patriotic ire was evidently aroused when Russia lofted Sputnik in 1957; commenting from one of his hamburger stands, he was quoted as suggesting that the sign on Russia's Sputnik factory ought to read "Washington slept here." As a symbol for the success and durability of capitalism, McDonald's soon attracted top government attention, and a year later Ray Kroc traveled to Washington at the invitation of Defense Secretary Neil McElroy to attend a "civilian orientation conference" at the Pentagon. He subsequently flew to West Berlin as representative at a government-sponsored agricultural exhibition.

The cold war would remain indelibly stamped on McDonald's fabric. Ray Kroc made the flag and flagpole a mandatory part of the franchisee's sign package. The owner-operator of his stands would also be offered the choice of a patriotic decor built around a huge, shiny plastic eagle with mighty wings and glazed, fierce-looking eyes. A banner streamed from its beak:

McDONALD'S. THE AMERICAN WAY.

But the boom in franchising was hardly confined to fast food. Being new, the system was above all promotable. Some of the razzmatazz and hoopla was reminiscent of Ray Kroc's Florida land-boom days. At times, any of the dozens of franchise shows that traveled the country resembled a carnival midway, offering every conceivable product and service. "We're dealing with an emotion second only to Hugh Hefner's —to own your own business," remarked Al Lapin, a former Los Angeles catering truck operator who in 1959 had launched his immensely successful International House of Pancakes. "And if I can find out how to franchise sex, I'll really have it made," Lapin told *Newsweek* in 1969.

Sex was not mentioned much in the new business gospel but just about everything else found a place in the franchise ads, inserts, and flyers that Americans discovered in their mailboxes and magazines during the sixties. In Nashville, Tennessee, two

funeral directors launched a skyscraper-mausoleum franchise
for "be-your-own-boss" undertakers. A Sacramento physician
offered a franchise method for sewing hair to bald scalps. The
Merlite Presto Shine Corporation of New York enticed prospects with a "remarkable patented invention," a polishing
machine. Goubaud de Paris Glamour Centers offered franchised wigs and cosmetics. A new hamburger chain urged,
"Put meat in your investment portfolio." "Let us send you a
Sheraton Motor Inn," casually suggested Sheraton Inns.

The variety and number of franchises for sale were truly
astounding: ice cream, burglar alarms, coin-operated laun-
dries, household pets, bridal accessories, whirlpool baths, "Mr.
Sharp" sharpening centers, and highly automated movie
houses. A buyer could obtain a Miss American Teen-ager
franchise from New York's Palisades Amusement Park. Folk
singers, elegantly attired butlers, chefs, and maids could be
had in one "package deal" from the Call-Arthur-Treacher-
Service franchise. And for the more adventuresome, a franchise
could be bought from Pacific International Limited dealing
with enuresis (bedwetting) among adults and children.

Founded by Robert Stearns in 1968, a trim fifty-two-year-old
outdoorsman, Pacific International franchised the sale of an
electronic device called "Nite-Dri," subsequently renamed the
"Little Watchman." According to *The Franchise Boom*, by
Harry Kursh, Stearns sold the franchise by traveling across the
country and holding meetings, complete with a motion-picture
projector and a zippy sales pitch citing names, dates, and
places of the Little Watchman's triumphs. Reportedly, Stearns
never failed to mention that one of his satisfied customers was
the nephew of a prominent member of Eisenhower's cabinet.
He then is said to have hired twelve salesmen and sold three
thousand contracts worth over $500,000 in income.

At the peak of the franchise craze, the nation's newsracks
groaned under the load of magazines containing glowing accounts of success stories similar to Stearns's. "For Harrie
Eisner," read a typical story, "the big change in his life came

when a cousin told him about something called Lawn-A-Mat, a tractor-like machine that sprays, seeds and rolls lawns all at once, doing a day's work for ten men in fifteen minutes." Another franchisee who signed up with General Business Services insisted: "I figure that I've added five or six years to my life by taking control of my own destiny." A man who had been ousted by his previous employer and decided to sell fifteen-cent hamburgers, remarked jubilantly, "Now I make more money than the president of the company that fired me. And here I'm the president, the chairman of the board, and the man giving the orders."

But as the sixties drew to a close, much of the rosy bloom evaporated overnight. As was typical of America's chaotic, boom-bust market conditions, a "shake-out" occurred in 1969. Scores of franchise companies fell by the wayside, along with millions of hard-earned and anxiously saved franchisee dollars. Tremendous overexpansion, shady operators, fast buck artists, and a host of fraudulent practices came to the fore with depressing regularity in testimony before Small Business Committee hearings in the House and Senate. By the early seventies the franchise industry was subjected to a dozen federal and state investigations that centered primarily on the lack of disclosure and complex clauses that faced the franchise investor. Only companies as solid and solidly run as McDonald's were to survive.

A representative story of the other sort of company was that of a man who put his $12,500 in savings into an A-to-Z Rentals franchise and then got stuck for every penny of it when the company went under in 1969. "There were thousands of [such men] in franchising a few years ago," commented *Dun's* three years later as it surveyed the wreckage. The story of A-to-Z Rentals, which used Johnny Carson's *Tonight Show* sidekick Ed McMahon as it promotional figurehead, was explained by a New Jersey dentist before Senate hearings on the Impact of Franchising on Small Business.

"Here was an outfit," the dentist recalled ruefully, "that

went out and sold an idea to, let's say, one hundred people, who paid an average of $10,000 each as down payments for their franchise. With the $1 million in the bank, they went 'public.' A million shares were sold at $13.75 each. With over $14 million, they embarked upon an aggressive program of corporate acquisitions, buying up one company after another within a year's time. . . . Within twenty-one months of going public they declared bankruptcy."

Some franchisors terminated a franchise simply so they could sell it again to a new dealer, allowing the collection of a whole new set of franchise fees. In the fast-food field, some reported huge earnings before a single outlet was opened by adding up the franchise fees. Stories were rife of sudden cancellations of contracts and of franchisees who found advertising claims, sales projections, and profits promised by the franchisor to be vastly exaggerated at best.

The situation was aggravated by the 1970 recession. By the middle of that year, *The Wall Street Journal* commented: "Once considered the darling of Wall Street and the savior of the small businessman, franchising today is spurned on Wall Street and cursed on Main Street." At least one hundred franchise companies were expected to go on the rocks. Even outfits like Al Lapin's International Industries and Bonanza International were said to be in trouble. The unsavory odor emanating from the once-luscious fruits proved embarrassing to the older, more established franchise concerns in the fast-food field.

Their chief lobby and spokesman, the Washington-based International Franchise Association, alerted its Boston College Franchise Center as early as 1966, resulting in the creation of an "action committee" to deal with the "fringe element" which, it was feared, "could give the entire industry a bad name." Three years later, Robert M. Dias founded the National Association of Franchised Businessmen to protect franchisees, and in its first three months of operations Dias reported receiving more than twelve hundred complaints. It was suggested during Senate hearings that franchise advertising and prospectuses, with their frequent misstatement of resources and earnings, should become subject to the rules set by the Securities and Exchange Commission.

At the height of the small business stampede in 1968 the U.S. Post Office also expressed its alarm. "The higher-quality crooks always take advantage of a successful, legitimate form of business," noted the chief postal inspector. "These days it's the boom in franchising." Of particular concern to the Post Office, state legislatures, the Federal Trade Commission, SEC, and various other government agencies were the doings of "pyramid builders" on the wild franchise frontier.

The key in the pyramid scheme was selling distributorships that would recruit other distributor-franchisees. Income was generated not by selling a product directly to consumers but by the recruitment of distributors who in turn recruited still more distributors. Each new franchise paid a cash fee that went to the top of the "pyramid," a method reminiscent of the hoary chain letter. Once the organization was built, its broad but flimsy foundation collapsed, leaving its organizers wealthy and the "distributors" broke.

Business Week estimated in the fall of 1972 that there were at least 125 separate pyramid operations in the United States. Donald Keith Wedding, a business professor at the University of Toledo, graphically demonstrated how the endless chain of recruitment was doomed by mathematical impossibility. He pointed out that if each distributor recruited five persons, each of whom recruited five more, there would be thirty million persons involved by the sixteenth level. By the twentieth level it would exceed the world population, and if each participant put up $5,000, there wouldn't be sufficient money in the world to build the pyramid to the twenty-first level.

A top pyramid builder was William Penn Patrick, who in 1964 at age thirty-three founded the internationally known Holiday Magic, Inc. A former door-to-door cooking utensil salesman from Illinois, Patrick's legendary rise to millionaire status began as he passed by a garage in San Rafael, California. He smelled something. Following his nose, he discovered that inside the garage were boxes and boxes of fruit-scented cosmetics. After buying the whole inventory and founding Holiday Magic, he decided to sell not the cosmetics but the cosmetic *distributorship*. Eventually Patrick built up a legion of distributors spread through four hundred subsidiaries, the vast majority of which one FTC official characterized as consisting mainly of the incorporation of "a secretary and a desk."

Patrick explained his gigantic scheme as "free enterprise personified." A political neanderthal on the far fringes of the lunatic right, he sought the Republican nomination for California governor in 1966, losing to Ronald Reagan after spending nearly a half million dollars and polling 3 percent of the vote. When federal authorities investigated he claimed that the attacks were inspired by his conservative political creed, which had earlier prompted him to call for the hanging of Chief Justice Earl Warren and the tarring and feathering of former Defense Secretary Robert McNamara for their softness on Communism.

Investigators were particularly startled by Patrick's Leadership Dynamics Institute, a motivational training program (for a fee) for Holiday Magic distributors and executives. Students in this program related hair-raising stories of how they had been sexually abused and even tortured in closed coffins, in wire cages, and on crosses. In 1972 one of Patrick's subsidiaries burst into national news with the crash of one of his Spectrum airplanes into a Sacramento ice-cream parlor that killed twenty-two people. William Penn Patrick himself was killed a year later while flying a World War II P-51 Mustang, also owned by Spectrum Air.

Two men who had taken a Holiday Magic course started their own pyramid firms; one of these was William E. Bailey of San Jose, California, the founder of Bestline Products Corp., a distribution of cosmetics, food additives, and cleaning supplies; the other was Glenn Wesley Turner, thirty-nine, a one-time peddler of sewing machines to blacks and poor whites in the rural south. Turner's pyramid was to overshadow all others.

Turner set up his distribution the way he had seen it done by his mentor William Penn Patrick: a triangle with himself at the tip and a melee of distributors below. He sold his distributorships for $5,000 to franchisees, who in turn brought in people under them as subdistributors for $2,000; for an additional $3,000 they could become area directors. After having sold hundreds of distributorships, Turner finally decided to look for a product to distribute.

In the end, he picked mink oil because he had heard that it was the nearest thing to human skin oils. The Koscot Interplanetary line would eventually comprise about 130 mink-oil-based "kosmetics" (Kleansing Kream, Nail Kote, etc.), which were sold door to door by "beauty advisors" reporting to several levels of some thirty thousand distributors.

To some 500,000 people in eleven countries Glenn Turner said: "If you can lean down to tie your shoestrings, you can reach up and lace the stars." Such faith was more than necessary for the Koscot distributors, who were promised that they could make $100,000 a year. The attorney general of New York noted that this meant that the people in Turner's New York program alone would have to sell 50 million distributorships inside two years—*eight* for every man, woman, and child in the state.

In the spring of 1972, Glenn Turner electrified a meeting of Detroit distributors who had paid $5,000 each. "Pretty soon we're gonna sell everything in America," he announced. "We're gonna have five hundred companies, and every one of them will have a president. . . . You men are all gonna be presidents."

Turner then kneeled down and made a slicing motion over a young girl's head at the foot of the stage. He shouted, "I'd like to open your brain and take out everything except thoughts of love and greatness!"

Turner's message was simple: "I want to make everyone a

millionaire." He repeated this message before spellbound audiences in as many as four cities a day, seven days a week. The effect he had on his audiences resulted in the coining of a new word, "Turnerized."

The "leadership" for Turner's ambitious plans was to come from the ranks of graduates of a special course. It was called Dare To Be Great, or DTBG, a self-motivation course that came in a $5,000 briefcase, consisting of twelve cassettes and a tape recorder. DTBG was divided into four segments called "Adventures" ($300 to $2,000 apiece) and twenty chapters called "Orbits."

At the completion of all the "Adventures" and "Orbits" and after paying a good sum of money, the student had launched himself into the stratosphere of salesmanship: he could now go out and sell "Adventures" and "Orbits" to someone else at a commission of $2,000 per $5,000 full course. Thus each purchaser had to resell distributorships in order to recoup his $5,000 investment, broadening the base of the pyramid and overloading the structure as each distributor scrambled to get closer to the top.

Dare To Be Great was the most successful of all Turner's enterprises, contributing 65 percent of his total business volume. Its message could be heard in rented school auditoriums, Holiday Inns, and veterans' halls throughout the United States at high-pitched, emotionally charged GO (for Golden Opportunity) Meetings. "The Unstoppable Glenn Turner," as he billed himself, would generally run down the aisle at top speed buoyed by the cheers of his advancemen, "GO! GO! GO! GO! GUHREAT! MONEY! MONEY! MONEY! MONEY!"

The hucksterism that characterized the franchise boom was not confined to the "fringe element," as the International Franchise Association constantly pleaded. In the late sixties it entered the broad mainstream as a rush of showbiz and sports personalities attached themselves to one or other franchise, the "hottest" being those in fast food. Even Ray Kroc early spotted the connection between patties and pizzazz. "When you are in this business you are in show business," he was quoted as saying. "Every day is a new show. It's like a Broadway musical—if people come out humming the tune, then the show was a success."

What the celebrities had to offer was nothing but their million-dollar names. They possessed what established trademarks like KFC and McDonald's already had—instant identification and, above all, "drawing power." The new promoters looking for a gimmick settled on the entertainer as a familiar figurehead to launch products that were less important than the name. For those chains without a celebrity to boast of, the entertainment motif was stressed in different ways. "Others feed you fast, we feed you fun," bubbled Shakey's, a West Coast pizza chain with banjo-playing Gay Nineties waiters.

The franchise operations that christened their fast-food establishments with the names of the famous and glamorous exploded on the scene. Suddenly there were Tony Bennett spaghetti restaurants, Alice's Restaurant, Fats Domino's New Orleans Style Chicken, Yogi Bear Honey Fried Chicken, Al Hirt's Sandwich Saloon, Rocky Graziano's Pizza Ring, Roy Rogers' Roast Beef Sandwich, Frank 'N Stein with Haunted Ham and Monster Burgers, Broadway Joe Namath's night spots, Say Hey, Willie Mays, and soul singer James Brown's Gold Platter restaurants in Macon, Georgia.

"Everyone's trying to get into the act," complained then chairman of Kentucky Fried Chicken, Jack Massey. "These entertainers who don't know their way around the kitchen may find they're jumping out of the frying pan into the fire."

The celebrity-franchise boom took on its most bizarre aspects in a city that became known as the franchise capital of the United States. Deep in the heart of Country and Western, Nashville in 1969 was the headquarters for more than thirty-four franchise operations. Their rivalry was referred to locally as the "chicken war," since chickens were what most of them sold. Country and Western stars eagerly lent their names to the product. Eddie Arnold turned up as chairman of Tennessee Fried Chicken, for instance, while others like Tex Ritter and Jimmie Dickens joined the fray with a pop tune: "A chicken hasn't got a chance in Tennessee."

The most grandiose scheme was concocted by a thirty-eight-year-old attorney, John J. Hooker, an energetic promoter who had campaigned for governor in 1966. Although he lost the race, he believed, according to a *Newsweek* article, that he would eventually enter the state house "on the back of a chicken." In the end he chose as his vehicle not a chicken but a pleasant, warm-hearted political supporter who had campaigned for him during the gubernatorial contest. Her name was Sarah Cannon, the "howdee girl from Grinder's Switch," better known as Minnie Pearl, star of the Grand Ole Opry.

John J. Hooker had gotten up a plan to challenge Colonel Sanders' primacy in franchised chicken. Regarding KFC as the Coca-Cola of the industry, it was his avowed intention "to become the Pepsi-Cola." He decided to talk to the woman who had believed in his candidacy.

Like most of the people attracted to franchising, Minnie Pearl was apparently unhappy, despite the success of her showbiz career. She was getting older and tired. "I had gotten to the point where most people get after a while in show business," she later explained in Senate testimony. "They are tired of one-nighters, and they are tired of the continual pressure of making plans and making all the efforts that you make to try to meet the busy schedule of show business."

Minnie Pearl became the vanguard of what John Hooker called his "blitz theory." Within a few years he had sold over eighteen hundred franchises. The influx of money flowed out into a complex pattern. He invaded black communities with a joint venture with Mahalia Jackson "Glori-Fried Chicken."

Minnie Pearl personally met every franchisee, giving them a picture and an autograph that said "I care," while her partner plowed on. John Hooker changed the name of his business to

Performance System. Restlessly, he changed it again, to Dynamic Systems. He bought a two-hundred-franchise ice-cream scheme and started a child-care franchise operation. According to *Business Week*, at the end of his "blitz" he had recorded net losses of $30.8 million on *sales* of $30.7 million, leaving his thousands of franchisees with a lovely picture of Minnie Pearl with its touching inscription.

Nothing as flamboyant as the Nashville chicken war shook the realm of hamburgers, where McDonald's reigned supreme. But there were rumbles. Some of the franchisees were discovering that the dream of independence was far from what it had been cracked up to be; that they were not small independent businessmen but highly paid managers who often worked seventy hours a week, not infrequently with their wives or other family members. From the average stand they could expect to gross $50,000 to $70,000 a year—a goodly sum, despite the headaches and the responsibility. Nevertheless, by the late sixties some found their futures fraught with the same insecurity and doubt that they had sought to escape by coming under the McDonald's franchise shelter.

The company had always taken an ambiguous position on their future, and some of the oldtimers who had watched Ray Kroc move to the sidelines were worried about the new breed of hamburger executive whose concern for the bottom line seemed stronger than the inspiration of Horatio Alger.

Horror stories about small-time franchisees losing their fast-food outlets were rife. Competition in the field was stiffening and the entry of the giant food conglomerates made survival ever more precarious. Their position was illustrated by the action of Ralston-Purina, a powerful agribusiness company. Two of its top executives held the post of secretary of agriculture during recent administrations. In 1971 Ralston-Purina suddenly became disenchanted with the franchising concept and gave thirty days' notice to all of its 642 Jack in the Box franchisees. Ralston-Purina had simply decided to terminate its franchising program.

Kentucky Fried Chicken franchisees faced no less a threat from their parent company. In 1970 KFC had three thousand units in operation, boasting it had never had a franchise failure. Then, despite record sales, KFC's stock began to slip, and the company responded by buying back outlets from its dealers. KFC's president John Brown, Jr., jubilantly told a security analysts' meeting, "We'll make more profit from three hundred company-owned stores than we will from twenty-one hundred franchise outlets." Eventually, Brown said, he would like to go "all-company" and buy them all back.

Even the vintage A & W Root Beer Company, the oldest fast-food franchise, had been acquired by a huge conglomerate, the United Brands Co. (formerly United Fruit Corporation). A & W's outdated franchise agreements—requiring the franchisee to buy nothing more than the company syrup—had long depressed profit margins and growth. Lamenting that "A & W should be McDonald's today," United Brands chairman Eli M. Black started a facelifting drive to make a A & W's "burger family"—Papa, Mama, Teen, and Baby Burgers—as standard as the Big Mac and Quarter Pounder.

The turmoil in fast-food franchising had the result of leaving the big names more firmly entrenched than ever. In the classic pattern of monopoly extension, the weaker chains were driven out and the bulk of the business fell in the hands of a few. With the new profits from a larger market with fewer competitors, mammoth trademarks like McDonald's had the resources to launch a snowballing expansion campaign.

Flush from rising profits, McDonald's increased its share of the market through new openings of company-owned stands, as well as through repurchases of stands from franchisees. In 1968 the company owned outright 15 percent of the McDonald's outlets. By the next year this share had risen to 20 percent. At the same time the company could not as yet buy up all the franchises. Like the larger industrial corporations, Mc-

Donald's too suffered from the "managerial crisis," a critical shortage of trained personnel which Hamburger University was still unable to sufficiently reduce.

In 1968 Ray Kroc modified his erstwhile characterization of franchising; he now called it the *"updated* version of the American dream," apparently conceding that franchisees were far from autonomous entrepreneurs. McDonald's was gradually giving way to an elaborate bureaucracy of hamburger managers, like the steel, chemical, and rubber quartermasters in America's other big industries. Each year's new ranks of Hamburger U graduates brought the operation under stricter control, and some of Ray Kroc's old franchisees viewed these developments with apprehension. The hard work and capital of franchisees had nurtured McDonald's into the world's largest and most successful hamburger complex, but only a shortage of mid-level managers stood in the way of full-scale absorption of the one thousand independent owner-operators left.

By 1973 Hamburger Central had extended its grip over the internal ranks by owning 30 percent of the McDonald's outlets. In Washington, D.C., alone it descended in one fell swoop to buy up forty stands at the price of $25 million. The Chicago *Tribune* noted that McDonald's indeed saw its future in a shift to a chain operation. "Kroc," reported the *Tribune,* "expects that one of the factors in the gradual conversion of the business to a chain from a franchise operation will begin with repurchase of its own franchises as operators decide to *retire* [italics added]."

By the end of 1974 the trend toward a company-owned operation had even created deep concern among some of McDonald's own fiercely loyal franchisees. The drastic change in concept had been summarized by Fred Turner in a speech to a meeting of security analysts. "Company-owned stores," he acknowledged, "are more profitable, but remember—this is a relatively new business, and we are limited by the number of experienced staff people we can draw on. Any man with five years of experience is considered to be at a valuable level of experience and is to be prized." He added significantly, "That's why we are not in the hamburger business—but in the people business."

Not all the people in the business were happy with their lot. The system of "approved" suppliers was apparently the cause of some friction between franchisees and Oak Brook headquarters. The company justified its supply and purchasing network on grounds of "quality control" and maintaining "strict specifications," and for those who failed to keep up the consequences could be severe.

McDonald's general counsel, Norman Axelrad, testified before Senate investigators: "Across the country at any given time there might be about six to ten operators whom we feel are very definitely below standard." He confided that Hamburger Central employed an "A" to "F" grading system, explaining that many of the stores were run "not as well as we would hope."

An example of the corporation's methods: operators were instructed to buy a new bun board, the approved supplier of which was Prince Castle, with which Ray Kroc has had a close association for nearly forty years. "This bun board," Central's instructions read, "is absolutely necessary for the toasting of the heels."

The plight of the McDonald's franchisee as corporate captive was not unique in the industry but no champion existed to fight its cause. McDonald's and the fast-food giants, meanwhile, had their own powerful Washington lobby, the International Franchise Association, which argued against the voices in Congress and among the regulatory agencies that urged full disclosure of the franchisor-franchisee relationship.

The franchisees needed a fearless fighter who could articulate their grievances—a Ralph Nader of franchising. They found this man in Harold Brown, a partner in the Boston law firm of Brown and Leighton, who took on the entire franchising industry—from Dunkin' Donuts to the Chrysler Corporation.

Brown's book, *Franchising: Trap for the Trusting,* had in-
furiated the International Franchise Association, which responded by publishing its own account of the industry, entitled
Franchising: the Odds On Favorite.
Brown's success in defending franchisees won him notable
acclaim. He was the author of the franchise fair-dealing bill
that was adopted in Massachusetts. He had investigated the
franchise method of distribution and had located the central
switch by which he claimed the parent company put the
squeeze on its operators: the system of supplies. In the case of
one pizza chain, for instance, he noted that court decisions
found that the company's franchisees had to pay 600 percent
over normal prices for ingredients.

According to testimony by Brown the Howard Johnson
chain, grandfather of the roadside restaurant, made no royalty
charges but received all of its profits from the seven hundred
items sold to its franchisees. A high markup and strict supervision of purchases through a web of company inspectors
enforced purchase of the products. In the case of a gallon of
maraschino cherries costing $1.50, for instance, the Boston
attorney charged that Howard Johnson simply changed the
label and priced it at $4.50.

"Shakey's charged $21.50 for the spice blend which costs
them $3," testified Brown. "Most Shakey's and McDonald's
prescribe that their franchise agreements are confidential, with
disclosure ground for termination. . . . It would be interesting
to obtain full disclosure as to the exact relationship between
McDonald's and such approved purveyors," he noted, "since
this relationship is pregnant with the risk of kickbacks." However, Brown's testimony has apparently not been acted on.

In order to pacify the growing restlessness in its own ranks of
operators, McDonald's launched an internal reorganization
drive in 1973. Its object was to forestall the type of insurgency
plaguing others. Organized under the Public Affairs Department, the corporation created the Operators Advisory Panel, a
company-sponsored association hastily set up to prevent the

establishment of a group organized independently by rebellious operators. The aim of the OAP, said Hamburger Central's internal newsletter, was to further develop communication between the home office and field.

The man put in charge of the Public Affairs Department was McDonald's general counsel and top spokesman, Norman Axelrad. He frequently travels to Washington and different state capitals to pump hands and tell the McDonald's side of the franchise story. Axelrad personally visits "problem operators." He is the soft-spoken man who appears, as if by magic, at the mere hint of contractual infractions. Axelrad calls it "jawboning," and when this fails, he points out that Hamburger Central has "the legal leverage to say 'either you sell out or we will bring an eviction action.'"

Axelrad describes the function of his Public Affairs Department as essentially "the monitoring of the political and social systems that exist in the world outside the corporation." He feels that good corporate management requires planning ahead, contingency planning. "At the risk of sounding a little corny," he explained, "maybe Public Affairs is directed at the preservation of the *bottom line.*"

The *bottom line*—the magic margin of profits—was also what Attorney Harold Brown had in mind while testifying during the 1973 hearings on "The Role of Small Business in Franchising" before the House Permanent Select Committee on Small Business. Singling out McDonald's as the "cynosure of the industry," he began to enumerate the various techniques employed by the company to mine its twenty-year hamburger franchises.

"Each of its franchisees," Brown asserted before the committee "must deposit a $15,000 security fund for which he receives a promissory note, *non-negotiable, non-interest-bearing,* payable in fifteen years, 50 percent, and in twenty years the balance of the 50 percent. So that with the two thousand franchises . . . McDonald's holds and intermingles with its own funds, $30 million for a period of twenty years. . . .

"A little mathematics," Brown continued, "will demonstrate at a very low rate of interest of 5 percent per annum, at the end of twenty years that would multiply to $40 million. But I can assure you that McDonald's does not work on a rate of return of 4½ or 5 percent per annum. . . . Mr. Chairman, at the end of twenty years on a 20 percent return, that $30 million is worth $120 million."

The attorney then sought to demonstrate to the congressmen how McDonald's made money on every transaction, at the expense of the franchisee who paid for the company's growth. "He pays a very substantial markup on the sublease of the premises," Brown explained. "He pays through the nose a profit on the equipment which he must purchase, and he is also required to pay a percentage of his gross sales as a royalty."

Brown made a quick numerical check on the fingers of one hand. "I count that he has been roasted and toasted five times so far!"

Donald McDonald
and Little Mac

"I Guess We Turned Out to Be a Rather Strange Bunch"

In March of 1971, according to the *Chicago Tribune,* three serious, soberly dressed Japanese students showed up in the portals of Hamburger U. They were Yoshaiki Katoh, Shigekazu Ohno, and Akuji Izuka. All were in their early thirties, they had all been previously engaged in selling, and they had come to Elk Grove Village to learn how to make a lot of money. "That's the name of the game," the dean said as he welcomed them to school.

Katoh, Ohno, and Izuka spent three weeks at Hamburger U. A $3,000 booth with a translator had been especially installed for their benefit. They sat in the lecture hall and stood behind the grills wearing "Trainee" hats. They studied the fifty-second patty, QSC/TLC, and computer fries. They learned the proper way of drawing shakes, of filtering water and deflecting grease. Katoh, Ohno, and Izuka studied all the elements of hamburger technology, except Big Mac.

The omission of McDonald's double-decker, triple-bun

monster from the Japanese program of hamburger studies was the result, according to the newspaper, of Hamburger Central's finding that the average Japanese stomach was "fifteen years behind that of its American counterpart." Katoh, Ohno, and Izuka therefore mainly concentrated on the standard patty on a bun, since it was better suited to their consumers. Later the Quarter Pounder would also be withheld from Japan for the same reason. Katoh, Ohno, and Izuka studied "Little Mac," Big Mac's junior partner.

After three weeks the students took leave of the dean. They apparently knew the name of the game. They smiled politely. They had a last look at McDonald's current company slogan: "Hamburgers by the billion add up to dollars by the hundreds of million." Then, with their B.H. degrees packed in their cases, they returned to the land of the Rising Bun, where shortly they reported to a chubby forty-six-year-old sales dynamo by the name of Den Fujita.

"Call me Den," reads his calling card.

Den Fujita is the president of McDonald's Co. (Japan), Ltd.—a joint venture between Hamburger Central, which controls 50 percent, and the Daiichiya Baking Co., Ltd. and Fujita Co., Ltd., each owning 25 percent. An importer of American luxury items, Fujita ate his first McDonald's hamburger in 1968 at a California stand during one of his frequent business trips to the United States.

The taste left him cold. More interesting, he felt, was the technology behind the hamburger.

Like Ray Kroc in San Berdoo two decades earlier, Den Fujita apparently was impressed by all he observed in that brightly lit McDonald's stand: the value, speed of service, the elimination of wastefulness, the cleanliness—in particular the money he could see churning in the till. The modern management and retail methods he saw applied seem to have intrigued him and turned his thoughts to Japan's own huge market, which consisted of over a hundred million people, newly affluent and with a consumer passion unrivaled anywhere.

The Japanese spent $10 billion a year on a chaotic clutter of restaurants, mostly of the Mom and Pop variety that on the average took in less than $100 a day. As he finished eating his hamburger, Den Fujita must have perceived a field that was still largely untouched by Japan's mammoth trading cartels. Hamburger and french fries. Simpler, faster, than rice and noodles and bowls and chopsticks.

Den Fujita was not alone in realizing that American-style fast food might be better suited than traditional eating habits to the pace of Japan's highly industrialized economic life. Since the end of World War II, the Japanese diet has become increasingly westernized. But the interest of the American quick-meal giants did not properly kindle until 1970, following the Japanese decision to liberalize the laws governing the operations of foreign companies. Faced with an American trade war, Japan agreed to implement additional voluntary restraints in exports. It also agreed to give American companies a bigger slice of the Japanese market, and among the first retailers allowed to operate freely were the U.S. fast-food marketeers.

Like latter-day Marco Polos, they swarmed over the archipelago. In early 1970 *International Commerce* reported the return of a typical U.S. trade mission to Japan. Three of the five executives were from Dunkin' Donuts, Burger King, and Carvel Ice Cream. Soon the big U.S. food conglomerates, eager to establish a toehold in a potentially huge market, set up their familiar roadside signs in Japan's big population centers: General Foods with Burger Chef; United Brands with A & W Root Beer; International Multifoods with Mister Donut; Heublein with Kentucky Fried Chicken; International Dairy Queen; Pizza Hut; McDonald's, Denny's Coffeeshops; Hardee's, Shakey's, and the rest.

The invasion of pizzas, ice cream, burgers, donuts, and

chicken came at a time when Japan was undergoing its first confrontation with large-scale consumer unrest. Housewives demonstrated against the high cost of living; newspapers bristled with reports of environmental damage and pollution. But some of the fiercest criticism was reserved for the quality of the Japanese diet. Nutrition experts, doctors, and consumer advocates charged that it had declined to dangerous levels. The Japanese people learned that the fish and rice they ate were contaminated. They discovered whole villages suffering from mercury- and cadmium-related poisoning. They heard the stuff they chewed and swallowed described as *kogai,* a "public hazard and environmental disruption." And when Den Fujita opened his first McDonald's in July, 1971, the Japanese flocked in virtual worship to the Golden Arches, to the QSC/TLC of the promised stand.

Den Fujita chose the site for his first store in the Ginza, Tokyo's commercial and entertainment center. The walkup establishment stood on some of the highest-priced land in the world, and at a time of galloping inflation the mere "value" of its eighty-yen (thirty cents) patty assured its success. Den opened two more stands in the next few months. After fifteen months there were fourteen, averaging $47,000 per month, compared to $40,000 then averaged by stands in the United States.

Fujita confidently predicted three hundred Japanese Mc-Donald's within a few years. He began thinking of introducing Japanese-style fast foods, such as instant *kitsune udon* and instant *onigiri,* traditional noodle dishes. He opened a Japanese Hamburger University in Tokyo's student district of Ochanomizu. To accommodate the Japanese tongue, he changed the name of Ronald to *Donald* McDonald. His two-fold mission was to reeducate the Japanese palate and to overcome the ancient Japanese taboo of *tachigui,* which proscribes eating while walking or standing.

Den Fujita saw his efforts crowned by becoming known as the "Hamburger King of Japan." And he staunchly attributed

McDonald's success in Japan to the fact that the company had a "Japanese head," an alliance sought by most American food franchisers when they decided to cross the Pacific. Burger Chef, for instance, which had decided to do without the "Japanese head," had soon found its American body unable to move. The vast majority of American fast feeders followed the example of McDonald's and Fujita. When Dairy Queen set up shop, for instance, it took a fifty-fifty share with the Giant Marubeni Corporation, while Kentucky Fried Chicken engaged in a similar joint venture with Mitsubishi, Japan's most powerful trading cartel.

Mitsubishi's resources of capital and market control enabled KFC to become the front-running American fast-food dispenser in the country, easily surpassing McDonald's. KFC opened its first two Japanese stores in 1969 and, following its phenomenal success at the Osaka World Fair, expanded quickly to some eighty-five stores three years later. The familiar figure of the world's biggest chicken salesman stood in front of the stands in the form of a life-size plastic Colonel Sanders holding a plastic box of plastic fried chicken.

Kentucky Fried Chicken led the American fast-food invasion abroad. With his white mane and goatee, the Colonel established beachheads in an amazing number of places. In less than a decade he ringed the world with over four hundred and fifty installations in over twenty-two countries. There were two in Nairobi, over one hundred in Britain. The Colonel could be found in Hong Kong, Tokyo, Melbourne, and Stockholm, and sometimes he was regarded with suspicion. In fact, German suspicion of Harland Sanders' wartime role, according to *Business Week*, was one reason for KFC's poor sales in that country. Similarly, two Russian correspondents who traveled the United States last year were also disturbed by the militarized chicken salesman. In a series of articles for *Pravda* they wondered whether the Southern gentleman had been given his rank for war-connected culinary services.

McDonald's had always trailed the Colonel until the May,

1973, issue of *Advertising Age* indicated a change in relations between the two fast-food giants. "Ronald McDonald has outpaced the Colonel," the trade paper announced, and even though KFC still had hundreds more outlets, McDonald's 1972 sales of $1.3 billion for the first time surpassed those of Colonel Sanders'. Thus, when McDonald's moved abroad, its strategy was to outflank the better-entrenched Kentucky Fried Chicken. Already well established in Canada, Costa Rica, Puerto Rico, and the Virgin Islands, Ray Kroc had followed the Colonel to Europe, and in the spring of 1971 McDonald's arrival on the Continent had been hailed by the almost simultaneous sprouting of Golden Arches in Holland and Germany as well as down under, in Australia.

A number of domestic factors contributed to the franchise exodus that saw some two dozen American chains move abroad along with McDonald's and KFC between 1969 and 1972. Among them were a number of service retailers, such as Snap-On-Tools, Duraclean, Manpower, and H. and R. Block; as well as hotels, such as the Holiday and Ramada inns. But leading the flight from home shores were the familiar trademarks of the American quick-meal giants.

Rising food and labor costs played a large part in the exodus along with the conditions of an increasingly crowded home market and a stiffening of competition. In 1972 *Dun's* warned that the American fast-food bonanza had "already run into the twin specters of market saturation and dwindling site locations." And as it became clear that the big super-profits lay elsewhere, A & W opened more than two hundred franchises overseas, with another thousand planned for such distant places as Tahiti, Hong Kong, and Singapore. Smaller chains, such as Sandy's, went into Belgium. There was a Bob's in Rio de Janeiro and Jack in the Box went into a joint venture with one of Europe's largest catering and restaurant concerns.

"I don't believe in saturation," Ray Kroc said. "We're thinking and talking worldwide." Both franchising and fast food were relatively new in Europe, and McDonald's transatlantic buildup proceeded rapidly. The stainless-steel grills were imported from the United States, as were the standard specifications, the hamburger technology and the patty production line.

France was one of the first European countries to become acquainted with Big Mac, where it was pronounced "Gros Mec." The French learned about "Gros Mec" through Janet Lynn, a young ice skater on the American team at the 1968 Winter Olympics in Grenoble. When she said, "The thing I miss most over here is a good American hamburger," the remark threw Hamburger Central's PR agents back in Chicago into a frenzy of activity, and within hours an Air France jet was aloft with four hundred hamburgers packed in dry ice. The cost was well worth the publicity, according to Hamburger Central's tireless propagandist, Al Golin. "We got all kinds of mention on ABC's coverage of the Olympics." But a few years later, after McDonald's opened its first stand on Paris's Champs-Elysées, the name Gros Mec was quietly abandoned. It turned out to be French slang for "big pimp."

Germany was treated to a similar show when Al Golin dispatched a special envoy with the mission of presenting a hamburger to the mayor of Hamburg. The city official appeared pleased but puzzled. "Hamburger?" he said, shaking his head. "Hamburger? *Ich bin ein Hamburger!*" In the fall of 1974 curious Londoners watched Ronald McDonald open the first stand in the United Kingdom. It was the only store in the worldwide chain to serve tea. A year later McDonald's debut in Stockholm was a bit more eventful. Bombs went off in two stands, set off by Swedish leftists to thwart what they called "creeping American cultural imperialism."

Until McDonald's invasion of the Continent, the American-style burger in Europe had catered mainly to snob-appeal and well-filled pocketbooks. At Le Drugstore in Paris, the Great American Disaster in London, and the Hollywood in Madrid, America's quick-meal staple was the favorite of the smart set, from Vatican ambassadors to movie stars. But McDonald's brought the burger to the European masses, and as it Americanized their eating habits, the uniform patty also took on a dash of continental flair. Wine was served with Big Mac in France, the Germans wanted beer. The Dutch liked theirs with applesauce, while the Austrians missed their own hamburger's customary tomato and beetroot. The Italians proved hardest to convince. One, a young Roman student, said he tried hamburger once. "It's better for cats," he was finally quoted.

But whatever its quality, McDonald's bland burger rolled on over all gustatory opposition. McDonald's could capture a market by selling its hamburgers for less. Its size enabled it to postpone profits while conquering new sales territory. Its huge resources of capital allowed it to make costly mistakes, such as initially opening most of its stands in the suburbs when it began operations in Europe. In England it could outsell the native Wimpy burger, which was more expensive. In Japan, where retail beef prices were twice as high as in the United States and rising by more than 30 percent a year, McDonald's could line up steady supplies of beef and tons of Idaho potatoes.

When McDonald's opened its flag-bedecked International Division at Hamburger Central in 1969, it expressed optimism that the basic approach that built the chain in the United States could be duplicated abroad. Hamburger Central counted on its massive system of control to back up its foreign operations.

But it did not quite work out that way in Japan, where often the "Japanese head" did not respond to control.

Today there is a McDonald's hamburger stand in downtown Hiroshima, near where the first atom bomb exploded. There's a Mr. Donut shop as well. The people of Hiroshima have taken to eating American-style hamburgers and donuts. Business is brisk. But to the present generation of Japanese business people, the current alliance with American business is still vividly rooted in Japan's military defeat in World War II. "Japan surrendered unconditionally to the United States," Den

Fujita says simply. The owlish, bespectacled chief of McDonald's Japanese operations also sees the current status of "Little Mac" as a reflection of the military reality, but he also shares a view of history that does not exclude the possibility of replacing American hamburger hegemony. "If we eat hamburgers for a thousand years," Fujita said in an interview, "we will become blond. And when we become blond—we can conquer the world."

Conflict and hostility have followed Fujita's attempts to sell the Little Mac to the Japanese people. On one front, his military behavior was said to have caused concern in the open office of Hamburger Central's International Division. With a pair of field glasses he kept on his desk, he would look out from his sixth-floor Ginza office to survey his McDonald's stand a few blocks away. In a May, 1973, article *Forbes* magazine called him a "bull in a hamburger shop," and reported: "Fujita's outspokenness and braggadocio-style of operating have earned him the ill will of many of his fast-food colleagues."

Not long after opening his first hamburger stands, Den Fujita seems to have found himself involved in conflict from all sides. Japan's Communist party charged McDonald's with "imperialism." A Tokyo department store executive, apparently angered at Fujita's manner, refused to lease McDonald's a site. Even Daiichiya, Fujita's bun-baking partner, began selling buns to competitors. At the same time, Den Fujita was locked in combat with a variety of native copycat hamburger chains, a crazy rivalry that Tokyo's newspapers would chronicle through the spring of 1973 as a full-scale "hamburger war."

McDonald's and Den Fujita burst on Japan's national scene almost immediately after the arrival of the Golden Arches. The confrontation took place in Chigasaki, a bedroom suburb of Tokyo, where McDonald's had opened a stand behind several large droopy trees. The trees were centuries old. They formed an umbrella that almost completely hid the store from view, and when McDonald's decided to chop them down, the issue became a rallying point for popular resistance. The anger grew after it was learned that McDonald's had tried to get the land ordinance changed so the trees could be removed. In an unusual show of unanimity, the major political parties lined up in a solid block against this.

Suburban Chigasaki was a location Hamburger Central had chosen in deference to McDonald's successful suburban formula. Fujita had disagreed vehemently, but the balking of the "Japanese head" was evidently disregarded. Fujita wanted to locate at the busy downtown sites, in the midst of Tokyo's metropolitan maelstroms. He argued loudly that the Japanese were not as motorized as Americans and that the Japanese suburbs were not the same focal centers of activity as those in the United States. But in the end, Fujita obeyed and selected the store, with its massive umbrella of ancient droopy trees.

Then Den Fujita did what he always did when there was a large-scale commotion. "I'd get hurt if I were to run around in a typhoon," he said, as the issue became a focus for a Japanese demonstration of sovereignty. "You've got to keep still when there's a typhoon around."

Den Fujita sat very still as the nationalist flak hit the Golden Arches. And Hamburger Central bowed to the Japanese head. It abandoned the suburb and meekly followed Fujita to the more profitable downtown sites, where a new typhoon soon raged.

Tokyo's "hamburger war" erupted following the Chigasaki incident. It began when McDonald's found itself trailed at every location by exact replicas of its own familiar mold. These homegrown Japanese hamburger stands, identical in every detail to McDonald's except the name, belonged to the Lotteria chain, owned by the Lotte confectionery firm. Long notorious for its unabashed imitations of American chewing gum and candy, Lotte's competitive zeal knew no bounds. When Den Fujita opened a new outlet in Yokahama's busy Isezakicho shopping district, Lotteria moved in on the same block with not one but two look-alike stands, as well as an offer of a free shake with the purchase of a hamburger.

Lotteria was only one of a half dozen local hamburger chains to harass McDonald's with copycat stands and names like Dum-Dum, Handas, and American Burger. From Tokyo they followed McDonald's to other cities—Nara, Kyoto, Osaka, Nagoya, Kawasaki, Chiba. A Japanese coffee company even began selling "Mac Hamburgers" through vending machines resplendent with the symbol of the Golden Arches. All of this was mere skirmishing, and by early 1973 the "hamburger war" was in full tilt.

It was fought with rumor, innuendo, and blaring slogans. Fujita reportedly charged his local rivals with using soybean extenders, horsemeat, whale meat, and fish meal. "Most big companies in Japan are stupid," he said, as the conflict heated.

But at the height of the hamburger war Den Fujita withdrew. There were still only thirty-two McDonald's stands in Japan, with another ten under construction. The country was racked by inflation and by shortages of building materials, even of beef. "McDonald's and the others thought they were sitting down to a feast," noted *Forbes* on Japan's fast-food boom and bust. "Many of them are ending up with indigestion."

While this new trouble was brewing, Den Fujita sat very still and penned a book that quickly became a best seller in Japan. Published in 1972, it was called *The Jewish Way of Doing Business*. A year later he authored a second book, also in praise of Jewish business acumen, *Dumb People Don't Succeed*. In Japan he became known in some quarters as the "Jew of the Ginza," but the only thing that seems to have surprised Fujita was that the books caused him to lose most of his Jewish-American friends whom he credits with having taught him the business methods that made him successful.

Fujita's interest in Jews was apparently kindled twenty-five years ago when he made his first buying trips to the United States. As an importer of American luxury goods, most of the people he dealt with, he said, were Jewish wholesalers and businessmen. He soon learned to admire them. "I have implemented in my daily work the methods of the Jews without myself being aware of it, I guess," Fujita explains. By traditional reputation Osaka's businessmen are said to be the shrewdest in Japan. Fujita, who is from Osaka, claims this is because Osaka's businessmen have Jewish blood in them.

Japan's Hamburger King believes that Hebrews came to Japan many centuries ago, and he has, he claims, found clues and evidences to support his theory.

Black Mac

"Ray Kroc Split So Fast He Left His Cane"

In the summer of 1972 Honolulu became the site of the largest gathering of Hamburger People ever assembled in one place. From all over North America, Europe, and Japan the hamburger people converged on the Hawaiian islands. Vice-President Jim Lynch of Hamburger U pulled into Honolulu at the helm of his own yacht, Ray Kroc flew in on his luxurious jet. Others came in festive charter parties. They met and mingled, fast-food fellows thrown together for three days of rediscovery, reminiscence, and renewed acquaintanceship. The occasion was the First International McDonald's Convention, an event the like of which would never be repeated.

People were strolling on Waikiki and cautiously dipping in the sky-blue ocean. They had arrived with pale and pink complexions, but on the second day they must have begun to brown. Wearing leis and Jantzens, bermudas and boaters and sandals and slacks, they paraded in groups through the hotel lobby and sat down at huge dinners to feast not on hamburgers, fries and shakes, but on herring in sour cream, escargots in garlic butter, baby spare ribs in sauerkraut, lobster bisque, frogs' legs with rice, and Belgian endive salad vinaigrette. There were some three thousand of them—managers, operators, and top-level executives. A hundred or so hamburger millionaires were sprinkled among the conferees. But for the many small-town and suburban managers and franchisees McDonald's First International Convention must have presented an occasion to exhibit the plumage of their newly won dollars. The women wore diamond rings on red-scrubbed fingers; their husbands were turned out in silk and brocaded suits. Conventioneers had a chance to talk to Fred Turner, who with characteristic energy was virtually everywhere, reportedly making peppy speeches urging everyone to sell more hamburgers. At night the Hamburger People danced and boomed along; the peppery Hamburger King is said to have tinkled old tunes on the piano.

The First International McDonald's Convention was not all frolic. Hamburger Central had chosen Hawaii's tropical setting and the occasion of the convention to unveil after years of testing the then latest addition to the patty pantheon, the Quarter Pounder.

The Quarter Pounder made its debut in Honolulu as a "Meal on a Bun" along with the solemn injunction that "man does not live by bread alone." Pictures of the Quarter Pounder abounded. A Broadway-style series of song and dance numbers reportedly introduced a parade of new machinery, plastic designs, and patty paraphernalia. A new hamburger commercial from Needham, Harper and Steers showed a kite getting stuck in a tree, a father and son working to get it out and eventually ending up at McDonald's. Stanley Beals, a vice-president at Needham, Harper and Steers, recalled there were tears when that commercial was shown.

Those present recall that many of the speeches consisted of testimonials to the moneymaking miracle of the McDonald's machine. Earnings were forecast, profits projected. The good cheer apparently increased.

Then Paul Harvey took the rostrum, while on the fringes of the convention a group of forgotten hamburger salesmen listened.

Paul Harvey, the descendant of five generations of midwestern preachers, is said to have looked a little like the late Everett Dirksen with a cold fundamentalist gleam behind his glasses.

Ray Kroc, a long-time friend and admirer, had invited Harvey to address the convention, apparently to give it a philosophical cast. Paul Harvey was articulate. As a news commentator with a largely small-town midwestern following, his reactionary flag-draped rhetoric could be heard over 462 American radio stations and 126 television stations and read in 300 newspapers. His news commentaries had been placed into the *Congressional Record* eighty-seven times. He had received six honorary degrees. Five hundred American communities had given him the key to their city. A Gallup Poll study in 1969 put him close to the top of America's "Most Admired" list.

His speech, according to people present, was a paean to free enterprise mixed with hoary clichés. Nobody was born with a silver spoon in his mouth. Everyone had to earn what they got. Those too lazy to work should reap the consequences. Nobody should expect something for nothing, and idleness and rioting was not going to solve any problems. That wasn't the American way, Harvey is said to have noted righteously.

And when he finished speaking, the fast-food fellowship dissolved, the cheer went flat. The forgotten hamburger salesmen appeared from the convention fringes. They formed the small, voiceless, and angry contingent of Black Mac.

Blacks had made a belated entry into Kroc's ranks of franchisees, yet the black ghetto stands happened to be some of the biggest money-makers in the chain. The black operators claimed to have many grievances, which apparently came to a boil at the First International.

The blacks were reportedly outraged by Harvey's speech and humiliated by the applause it received. Afterward, they sent a letter to Ray Kroc and other executives. Its authors were a small New York contingent of black operators led by the *only* woman operator in the McDonald's chain. Joined by black operators from Chicago and Cleveland, the group hastily formed a black caucus to protest Harvey's speech. Also hammered out was a draft of long-standing discontents. The black operators apparently complained that they were excluded from all participation in the decisions of Hamburger Central and accused the burger bureaucrats of failing to deal with their special problems. Oak Brook did not understand the needs of the black community. Operating a McDonald's in white suburbia was not the same as operating a stand in the ghetto, they said.

There would be no Second International Convention.

The genesis of the black capitalist was "enlightened" self-interest. Economic discrimination against black Americans and other minorities was recognized as a political powder keg. Government and business leaders realized that a completely dispossessed black population could become a breeding ground for revolutionary turmoil, as was demonstrated in Watts in 1965; in Newark and Detroit in 1967; and in the riots after Martin Luther King's assassination in 1968.

In 1960, during his presidential campaign against John Kennedy, Richard Nixon gave voice to the general fear of what a hopelessly mired black population, driven by desperation, might turn to. "Every act of discrimination," Nixon said, "was like handing a gun to the Communist." It was much the same concern that led the Johnson administration to launch its War on Poverty, a strategy fed by alarming figures which showed that between 1950 and 1960, black ownership of business had actually *declined* by one fifth. The few blacks that made it up the economic rungs were situated in professional and technical occupations. During the sixties the number of black managers and small business owners—despite much-ballyhooed promise —grew at a fractional pace.

The creation of the black capitalist was entrusted to a special federal bureaucracy, the Small Business Administration, which grew out of President Johnson's Office of Economic Opportunity. The SBA never pretended that it sought to deal with the deeply rooted social and economic causes of black poverty; its aim was small business pacification in response to the civil rights movement of the early sixties. It looked for a select few to become black figurehead Horatio Algers.

Never meant to institute serious reform, the SBA was used by successive administrations to soothe minority aspirations. Berkeley G. Burrell, former president of the black National Business League, noted sadly that the aim was to "offer Band-Aid type programs for our serious injuries" and after a few years of watching SBA operations, Burrell concluded that the plight of the black businessman was still no different from what it had been in the days of Booker T. Washington.

To usher in the promise of the black, or minority, capitalist, the SBA turned inevitably to the small-business franchise, the economic Miracle Whip that could give everyone, including Black Mac, a taste of being his own boss. SBA interest in franchising began under John F. Kennedy with a small outlay of $80,000 for the University of Minnesota to do a detailed study of franchising, which resulted in a report that drew the remarkable conclusion that a career in franchising could fulfill the "strong drive in most men to accomplish something of significance during their lifetime."

Even though a few officials in the SBA argued logically enough that a loan to a franchisee was in reality a loan to the franchisor, the agency's hurry to seed a small crop of black capitalists waived such considerations. Under the tactical direction of the SBA, franchising became part of LBJ's stockpile against the War on Poverty. As early as March, 1964, the indefatigable A. L. Tunick of Chicken Delight succeeded in convincing the U.S, Department of Commerce to set up a Task Force for Equal Opportunity in Business. The task force promised to devote special attention to "the availability of business opportunity for members of minority groups in the franchise field."

The SBA subsequently joined hands with major national franchise companies to sponsor shows and training courses in low-income areas; while matchmaking between the minority franchisee and national franchisor became the chief activity of another small office at the Commerce Department, the Affirmative Action Program, successor to the Task Force.

Flowery rhetoric and impressive code names accompanied the policy. Up until the Watts revolt, the number of blacks in franchising had been negligible, with even the second oldest and most important franchise business, new-car dealerships, having a total of one single black franchisee. As a result, a series of programs were rapidly established—and just as rapidly dismantled.

The Economic Opportunity Loan program was launched by the SBA in 1964 with a plan called "six-by-six," a loan of up to $6,000 for up to six years. This was followed by a program sponsored by the departments of Commerce and Labor called FTI (Franchise Training Institute), which succeeded in putting a few hundred minority youngsters to work in fast-food stands.

In 1967 came LBJ's "One-Stop Service for Businessmen," while the SBA "liberalized" its rules so that a franchisee no longer had to submit his franchise contract to the SBA for review, thus leaving the minority businessman completely at the mercy of the franchisor. At the start of the seventies, SBA's own survey of minority ownership in franchising—including blacks, chicanos, Indians, and Puerto Ricans—counted a mere 354 out of 27,000 outlets questioned. Brady Keys, former back for the Pittsburgh Steelers and president of All-Pro Chicken, the nation's largest black-owned franchisor, testified in January, 1970, at Senate Small Business hearings that the SBA minority franchise program had been "more of a boondoggle than a boon for small businesses and blacks." He also took bitter note of the SBA's abundance of rhetoric and matching lack of meaningful action.

The rhetoric reached its highest level during the 1972 GOP campaign, which installed the issue of minority capitalism as the centerpiece of Nixon's civil rights program. This plan had the unusual distinction of aiming not to win over blacks but to divide up the traditionally Democratic Mexican-American vote. Nixon's Committee to Re-elect the President (CREEP), under former Attorney General John Mitchell, had already devised a Southern strategy designed to sacrifice the black vote for the white Wallace support. But less known was CREEP's Southwest strategy, which abandoned the disappointing quest for the black capitalist in favor of the brown capitalist to sweep the important Mexican-American vote in Texas, Colorado, New Mexico, Arizona, and California.

It was Maurice Stans who had announced early in Nixon's presidency the rebirth of minority capitalism with a fanfare that exceeded anything in the past. And with hopes raised so high, the short fall was particularly bitter. For most blacks and chicanos who followed the pied piper of small capitalism, the tune became an entrapment, while the dapper, jauntily tailored Secretary of Commerce who had fed their dreams became a central figure in the Watergate affair.

"Any business is a risk," Stans acknowledged in a speech, "and a small business is the biggest risk. And it is certainly no secret that a minority business is the biggest risk of them all." Then he gave it the old cheer: "But the bigger the risk, the bigger the gain . . . the higher the odds, if you win, the greater the gain."

In October, 1969, Stans promised that he would try to get $300 million in federal grants, loans, and guarantees to aid minority business development. At the same time he gave the

Senate Small Business Committee a progress report on the
Commerce Department's Office of Minority Business Enterprise (OMBE) and its cryptically code-named "25 × 25 × 2"
program, which meant nothing more than that twenty-five top
franchise companies had been asked to create twenty-five
"opportunities." Stans also announced the goal of getting one
hundred minority dealerships from the giant oil companies
and the big four automakers. But, *The Wall Street Journal*
reported, "he could not produce any firm pledges from them."

By the time of the 1972 Nixon reelection campaign, the SBA
had been converted into a vehicle to steamroll nonwhite presidential support. Like the Justice Department, the IRS, FBI,
CIA, and other government bureaucracies, the SBA had become a politicized arm of the administration—a dispenser of
favors and a berth for loyal party workers. In testimony before
an investigating committee of the Senate Watergate hearings,
former White House aide William Marumoto related that the
goal was to "make sure the right people were being considered
and getting grants." Invariably, the nonwhite candidates for
upward economic mobility were loyal Nixon supporters.

One of the administration's most prominent blacks to be
groomed for capitalist status was Dr. Thomas Matthews, a
forty-nine-year-old neurosurgeon and a staunch Nixon sup-
porter. Nixon and Matthews had been introduced in 1966 by
Nixon's speech writer Patrick Buchanan, who recommended
the doctor's ideas about black capitalism as "meritorious."
Buchanan's observation took on poignancy after Dr. Matthews
was sentenced to a six-month jail term for tax evasion in 1969.
Though he was soon set free by a presidential pardon, Dr.
Matthews's conviction on seventy-one counts of illegal use of
Medicaid funds inspired an investigation of the SBA since
Dr. Matthews had handled about $11 million in federal funds
in his black capitalist program NEGRO (National Economic
Growth and Reconstruction Organization).

The investigation, however, ran into some unexpected obstacles. When Senate Watergate investigators asked for the

records on Dr. Matthews, *The New York Times* reported that the White House tried to get the SBA to burn its files. It also reported that during the *Times's* own investigation the Justice Department gave deliberately confusing "or even false answers about the material that was available on the doctor." In the end, the White House disclosed that former presidential counsel and key Watergate witness John Dean had referred the entire SBA file on Dr. Matthews to the Justice Department. The assistant White House press secretary explained Dean's unusual custody over the file as being due to "the President's strong interest in getting minorities in the mainstream of business."

Under the big business of Watergate, the small business of the SBA unfolded a similar pattern of corruption. In rapid order, twenty-two of its seventy-two field offices were singled out for investigation, and these soon began yielding a clearer picture of how the administration had used the SBA's minority capitalism program. In the fall of 1973, while calls for the President's impeachment were increasing, the Justice Department began an investigation of kickbacks and bribes that ended up in the hands of the special Watergate prosecutor. Among its findings, reported the *Christian Science Monitor,* were that the much-vaunted Office of Minority Business Enterprise systematically forced applicants to make illegal payoffs. A few months later the ranking Republican in the House hearings into the SBA called for the resignation of its chief, Thomas L. Kleppe, for failing "to clean up the mess of the SBA."

Prior to 1969 there were reportedly only five black franchisees at McDonald's, all of them in Chicago's inner city. But then, late in the year, the Cleveland ghetto exploded around the Golden Arches, resulting in mass demonstrations and a boycott of four McDonald's stands in the black neighborhoods. The Cleveland uprising forced a number of small accommodations, which in turn led the way for the cautious trickle of black operators not only in McDonald's but to all of the fast-food franchise industry.

The Cleveland boycott was fierce and bitter. The stands in the ghetto were all owned by the white franchisees, and the community's main grievance appeared to be that McDonald's took revenues out of the ghetto and gave nothing back. The community demanded black ownership of ghetto business, and with the scars of Cleveland's recent race riots still visible, Hamburger Central was persuaded to reach a settlement by urging its franchisees to sell out to a group of local black businessmen. Indeed one of the operators that McDonald's urged to sell out is suing McDonald's because of claimed breaches of agreements allegedly made by McDonald's to induce many to make such a sale.

The Cleveland show of black power forced a radical change in policy. McDonald's launched a program to sell white-owned outlets in black areas. Within two years fifty stands were black-owned, while a few dozen more applicants were on the waiting list. McDonald's warmed to the task after discovering that black ownership paved the path for further entry into the inner-city marketplace where profits were vastly higher than in most suburban stores.

In the poor black neighborhoods, the cheap mass-produced food was more than a snack. It generally constituted an all-purpose meal. Not surprisingly, a disproportionate number of ghetto stands belong to Hamburger Central's "million-dollar club," the restaurants which do over a million dollars a year in business.

Shortly after the Cleveland crisis, Hamburger Central also arranged a franchise for a West Side Chicago stand that came to be known for its "Better Boys Burger" and slogan—"Serve the People . . . Big Macs." The franchise was held by Westside Hamburger, Inc., which had been established by two nonprofit social service organizations—the Better Boys Foundation and the West Side Organization.

Originally a street-gang-oriented athletic club in the old

Archie Moore gym building in Chicago's ravaged, rat-infested North Lawndale ghetto, the Better Boys Foundation bought into a troubled McDonald's franchise. Yet within a few years it raised gross income to over $1 million—profits that went back into the foundation to serve the community with educational programs. Hamburger Central claimed it as an example of its beneficial ghetto presence. But the executive director of the foundation, Warren Saunders, pointed out in an *Ebony* magazine story that the McDonald's franchise was "really just a drop in the bucket" in terms of the total number of people affected and the money it earned to remedy some of the community's problems.

McDonald's move into the profit-ripe ghettos presented a host of problems for which the average Hamburger U graduate was ill prepared. As a result, six black Chicago operators with a total of thirteen McDonald's stands got together to form the Black McDonald's Operators Association (BMOA), which started its own black Hamburger U with a curriculum of Afro-American hamburger studies. Under BMOA prodding, Oak Brook ventured into black TV commercials. It appointed a special public relations supervisor and it engaged a black Madison Avenue–style advertising consultant, who is said to have assured worried hamburger executives that Ronald McDonald with his painted face and red afro wig was really colorless and acceptable to blacks.

But despite its general success in appeasing the surface demands for black control, Hamburger Central apparently failed to appreciate the depth of the new ghetto militancy. In some black neighborhoods in Chicago Ronald McDonald was reportedly chased, his red afro flying, by youngsters shouting, "Don't come back till you're black!"

No longer satisfied with Black Mac and Better Boys, one black Chicago labor organization demanded that Hamburger Central institute a scholarship program for its minimum-wage employees "so that a young worker won't just have a diploma from 'Chicken University' or 'Hamburger College' or 'French

Fried Institute.'" And the flames of anger fanned when a sudden unfounded rumor swept the West Side and South Side ghettos in the fall of 1973 that McDonald's was serving putrid meat in black neighborhoods.

The situation evidently caused an unusual spate of activity at Hamburger Central. It was potentially even more explosive than the nationwide black boycott threatened earlier. It was a matter that seemed to demand sessions of the highest burger body and intervention from the top. After a flurry of consultations, the Public Affairs Department decided that a number of black newsmen would be invited to Oak Brook headquarters and meet with chairman Ray Kroc. Placed in charge of the operation was McDonald's public relations firm, Cooper and Golin, which deputized an account supervisor to take the newsmen on a tour of the meat processing plants and Hamburger Central. The contingent rode on a Big Mac bus to Oak Brook. There they observed the space design, the open office, and the surreal clutter of artifacts before being led into the think tank. Then they proceeded to the boardroom, where Ray Kroc and top hamburger executives were waiting.

The talks snagged immediately on the issue of the open-neck shirt worn by one of the newsmen, Lew Palmer of Chicago's *Black X-Press*, who also had a daily radio program on station WBEE.

Ray Kroc seemed in an irritable mood, Palmer recalls. He lectured the visitors that in "the proper places" and at certain times it was necessary to wear a tie. "What would happen if there were no standards?" reasoned the Hamburger King. "Frankly," he told Palmer, "if you let a guy take his tie off, then next he'll want to take off his shirt, and where do you stop?"

Several executives apparently tried to calm the shouting match that followed but the meeting was over.

"Ray Kroc split so fast," Palmer recalled in amazement, "he left his cane."

After the conference, Lew Palmer returned to his office more convinced than ever that hamburger capitalism was merely tokenism. The next day his paper came out with a story headlined "X-POSE. HAMBURGER POWER. Blacks Just a Crumb from the Bun." In the article, Palmer urged his readers to keep a sharp eye on the inner-city exploits of McDonald's. He related his run-in with the Hamburger King and concluded poignantly:

"As I walked tieless away from McDonald Plaza, I looked back at this fantastic monument to hamburger power. And I couldn't help but think about the countless blacks who helped build it with their quarters and dimes and pennies, with which they bought what for many was a full meal—a hamburger, french fries and a Coke."

The Politics of Hamburger

"Mr. President, It's 12 Billion"

America's most American food actually had its origin in Russia. Medieval Tatars on the Russian steppes were the first to eat a primitive hamburger, which consisted of scraped raw meat seasoned with salt, pepper, and onion juice—what we know today as steak tartare. German sailors visiting the Baltic ports brought the recipe to Hamburg, where the ground meat was given its moniker, made into patties, and broiled, leaving the inside rare. The delicacy was brought to the United States in the early 1800s by German immigrants settling in the Cincinnati area. And it would reemerge in the fifth generation, a century later—"as American as a McDonald's hamburger on the Fourth of July."

But before the hamburger could evolve into the mechanized, mass-marketed McDonald's version, two other steps were to precede its incorporation into the diet of the American masses. From England in the 1880s came a popular cure-all prescribed by Dr. James Salisbury, who recommended that his patients eat cooked ground beef three times a day with a drink of hot water, a "medicine" that survives on restaurant menus as Salisbury steak. An even earlier contributor to the rise of the patty was the fourth earl of Sandwich; when the earl got hungry during a twenty-four-hour card game, he ordered two slices of bread and a slab of cold beef—and thus the "sandwich" was born.

Although the American hamburger is credited with having been born at the 1904 Saint Louis World's Fair, Chicago became its home. America's first hamburger chain, White Castle, is still in existence in Chicago today. Chicago was Meat City, ruled by the "kings of animal food" well before Ray Kroc was born. And Chicago was also the city where the politization of the hamburger first took place. None other than Richard Daley, America's most powerful mayor, received his first taste of political power through his work in an old South Side organization known as the Hamburg Club.

The members of the Hamburg Club were known as "Hamburgers," and the Hamburg Club would play a pivotal role in Daley's ascendancy. "If it never made *Who's Who in America*," wrote Mike Royko in his best-selling *Boss*, "it's part of what's what in Chicago."

Billing itself as a social and athletic organization, the Hamburg Club, according to Royko, sent aldermen, state legislators, city councilmen, and a pistol-packing congressman to office before Richard Daley became its president in 1924. The Hamburg Club was the most potent organization in the Thirteenth Ward, where Daley grew up. He joined in his teens, coaching the Hamburger softball team, and he would remain Hamburger president until the outbreak of World War II.

In later years, Daley would piously describe the Hamburg Club as a cross between the YMCA and the Boy Scouts, the same metaphor Ray Kroc chose to characterize his McDonald's chain. But the actual history of the Hamburgers was less placid. According to author Royko, the club in its early days was little more than a gang of street brawlers that "campaigned" for its favorite sons with old-fashioned muscle and threats. In 1919, during the worst race riots in Chicago's history, the Hamburgers, along with several other "athletic clubs," were blamed by an official riot study as being among the leaders of attacks on blacks that left thirty-eight dead and wounded.

Richard Daley became mayor of Chicago in 1955, just a few weeks after Ray Kroc opened his first McDonald's hamburger stand in nearby Des Plaines. In the same year, Oscar Mayer, the kingpin of hot dogs, died; also in 1955, as if to give expression to the rise of hamburger power, a heavily perspiring Lithuanian coal miner by the name of Philip Yazdik sat down and ate seventy-seven hamburgers at one sitting. (Yazdik said he could have eaten more but the photographers made him nervous.)

Richard Nixon had a long and fond association with the hamburger, which went back to his early youth. In his first quest for the presidency against John F. Kennedy, he boasted of his hamburger tastes as opposed to the presumably fancier fare enjoyed by his millionaire opponent. As the candidate whistle-stopped through the Midwest, writes David Wise in *The Politics of Lying*, Nixon emotionally recalled the little Whittier grocery store run by his parents. Because of the depression, customers would buy hamburger rather than steak, Nixon told one rally—"stew meat rather than chuck roast that was a little more expensive, no strawberries out of season."

But by the next stop the story had changed. The candidate, writes Wise, "was suddenly grinding the hamburger himself."

"You know," Nixon addressed the crowd, "one lady would come in and there would be nice hamburger. I ground it myself, incidentally—no suet in it, all meat—and it was mighty good, incidentally; only twenty-two cents a pound then —but there would be some nice hamburger, and over there would be a fine roast beef. So the lady would buy the hamburger, because she had a big family."

Nixon had a less happy association with hamburger shortly after his reelection as vice-president in 1956. The incident was related by Noah Dietrich in his book, *Howard: The Amazing Mr. Hughes,* and it came about in connection with a loan from Howard Hughes for Richard Nixon's brother Donald, who was then operating the Nixon Family Restaurant in Whittier. The establishment, which featured a sandwich called the Nixonburger, had been operating in the red for a year when Dietrich was ordered by his boss, Howard Hughes, to issue a $205,000 loan from the Hughes Tool Company.

Hughes Tool did a huge business in government defense contracting, and, realizing the delicacy of the operation, Dietrich traveled to Washington to advise Richard Nixon that the loan to his brother could have serious repercussions if it ever became known. "Mr. Dietrich," Vice-President Nixon is said to have replied, "I have to put my relatives ahead of my career." The high-powered executives of the Hughes Tool Company then made a number of recommendations to make the restaurant profitable. But this angered Donald Nixon, and again the vice-president was forced to intervene. "My brother wants to run it his way," he apologized to Dietrich.

The loan went through, the restaurant failed, and the $205,000 was never repaid.

The affair was reported by columnist Drew Pearson just before the election of John F. Kennedy. According to Robert Kennedy, the Hughes loan was one of the chief factors that swung the vote in his brother's favor.

The politics of hamburger was practiced with equal zest by the late FBI director J. Edgar Hoover. One of Hoover's longtime cronies in Washington was Harry Duncan, the owner of Little Taverns, a chain of hamburger joints that Ray Kroc got to know well during his years as paper-cup salesman. According to one of Hoover's friends, quoted by muck-raking author

Ovid Demaris, the FBI director, together with his inseparable second in command, Clyde Tolson, "made a lot of money investing in the Little Taverns."

Up until the mid-sixties, the politics of hamburger had remained largely anonymous. But with the advent of McDonald's it suddenly gained a name, as well as political prominence. On the campaign trail, hamburger began to edge the traditional chicken, and increasingly the hamburger was identified by name. During the 1974 California Democratic race for the gubernatorial nomination, one candidate estimated that he spent 75 percent of his meals during the campaign under McDonald's Golden Arches. "My opponents remind me of McDonald's hamburgers," charged Los Angeles Democratic gubernatorial contender Herb Hafif. "Instead of fast-food service, they are a fast-answer service. All programmed and uniform. Just like every McDonald's hamburger has pickles and onions and sauce. There are no alternatives."

In 1968, Ray Kroc, as chairman of McDonald's System, donated $1,000 to Richard Nixon. It was his first political contribution. The Hamburger King always seems to hold a jaundiced view of politicians, apparently suffering them as necessary evils who meddled with free enterprise, dispatched tax collectors and auditors from federal, state, and local levels, created zoning laws, countless regulations, and minimum wages. He called elections "popularity contests." "The first thing you do when you want to be elected is to prostitute yourself," he said cynically. "You show me a man with courage and conviction and I'll show you a loser."

But some four years and five billion burgers later, as Richard Nixon's reelection campaign got under way, Ray Kroc's opinion must have mellowed. In the four years of the Nixon presidency, Hamburger Central's revenues had nearly doubled and had gone beyond the billion-dollar mark.

At Hamburger Central Ray Kroc installed a framed quote from Richard M. Nixon called "Leaders Lead":

I have an absolute rule. I refuse to make decisions that some-body else can make. The first rule of leadership is to save your-self for the big decision. Don't allow your mind to become cluttered with the trivia. Don't let yourself become the issue.

Ray Kroc upped his donation to Richard Nixon from $1,000 in 1968 to hundreds of thousands in 1972. Newspapers gen-erally reported it to be in the neighborhood of $200,000. Jack Anderson wrote in his "Washington-Merry-Go-Round" that it was $255,000. One congressman put it at $208,000. Repre-sentative Elizabeth Holtzman of New York charged that it was $240,000. The Hamburger King himself remembers it as $250,000. Public records give the figure as $208,000, con-tributed in a short space of time with checks for relatively small amounts, most of which were payable to various state re-election committees.

Ray Kroc's generosity was apparently stimulated by his fears of a McGovern victory. He feared the Democratic presi-dential candidate as a disaster for business freedom—the right of any man to make as much money as he could and saw an accelerated creep toward socialism, which he felt Richard Nixon could stem. There was already too much government interference in business. There was enough of a trend this way, he said, "without having it become a radical type of thing."

"Your freedom is being diluted," Kroc claimed, "when they get so that they demand that you keep certain records for them. It means we've got to put one hundred people on our payroll. This is what I mean about the dilution of freedom—the freedom to run your own business."

Nobody more eloquently articulated Ray Kroc's feelings on the necessity of Nixon's reelection than the financial chief of the 1972 Nixon campaign. "Maurice Stans is a proven, high-class businessman," Kroc said admiringly of Nixon's commerce secretary and financial armtwister. "He's a very reputable man."

The Hamburger King met Stans during a special luncheon in early 1972 for big-time corporate chieftains and new-money business tycoons. Ray Kroc had been invited by the board chairman of the Quaker Oats Company. Maurice Stans had temporarily resigned as secretary of commerce to drum up what was to become the largest—as well as the most tainted—campaign treasure of any American election.

During the luncheon, Stans is said to have hammered away at the dangers threatening the country's business leaders. The United States, he reportedly said, was being faced with grave social changes that could lead to a highly socialized country. He said prosperous businessmen had an obligation to support the free-enterprise system, and he offered the example of religious groups like the Mormons who supported their church with generous tithes and donations. Then he made his pitch for Richard Nixon as the man to protect the interests of America.

"I think in all candor that you ought to put your money where your mouth is," Stans was quoted as concluding. "And I think that's a very small thing, but a great patriotic duty that you owe for the benefits that you've had."

After the speech, Ray Kroc went up to Stans. He had apparently been moved, stirred by the appeal to religious duty. He recalls pointing to his heart and declaring, "When you said 'put your money where your mouth is,' you hit me right here." Then he added prophetically, "I'm the kind of guy who is either going to do it or shut up. And I don't want to shut up."

Whatever the size of Ray Kroc's contribution, it placed him among the largest contributors and resulted in his invitation to the White House for a dinner with the President reserved specifically for the most generous. The black-tie affair was attended by the cream of American capitalism, including Henry Ford, computer millionaire Ross Perot, and construction tycoon Del Webb. Ray Kroc sat next to Ross Perot, whom he had met some time earlier when they were both given the Horatio Alger Award.

The highlight of the evening came before dinner, when

all the magnates and tycoons assembled to shake hands with the President. Somewhat shyly, Nixon moved down the line. When he came to Ray Kroc, he extended his hand and wiggled his finger.

"What is it now," Nixon asked, "eight or nine billion?"

"Mr. President, it's twelve billion."

The finger stopped wiggling; the two men grasped hands.

"My goodness," Nixon said, very pleased, "isn't that wonderful?"

On November '14, 1971, some eight months before Ray Kroc's White House dinner with the President, the McDonald's Corporation raised prices on the Quarter Pounder from fifty-three to fifty-five cents, and on the Quarter Pounder with cheese from fifty-nine to sixty-five cents. It did this at a time when the Nixon administration had instituted price controls during Phase 2 of its "economic stabilization" program; and not long after the "new" prices of the Quarter Pounders went up in thousands of McDonald's stands, the Price Commission, then a unit of the Cost of Living Council, ordered the increases rolled back.

The Price Commission ruled that McDonald's had raised prices in violation of control regulations, but its order that the company restore the original prices was forcefully resisted by Hamburger Central. And on July 10, 1972, McDonald's formally asked the Price Commission to cancel its rollback order and to exempt the Quarter Pounder and the Quarter Pounder with cheese from controls. On September 8, 1972, the Price Commission canceled its rollback order. In a complete reversal of its previous stand, it allowed McDonald's to raise the price on the Quarter Pounder with cheese by four cents, from fifty-nine to sixty-three cents—a 9 percent increase. It was an economically important decision that spelled millions of dollars in additional profits. A satisfactory explanation has yet to be made by the Price Commission.

The Price Commission's sudden about-face was seized on by the outspoken foe of the Quarter Pounder: Democratic Congressman Benjamin Rosenthal of Queens, New York, had already charged that McDonald's blockbuster burger misled consumers by weighing less than its name implied. Chairman of a House Consumer Task Force, the Queens congressman renewed his attack with a press release charging that McDonald's favorable Price Commission ruling had been bought with Ray Kroc's "massive campaign contribution."

Rosenthal ranked the Quarter Pounder case with the Soviet wheat deal and the ITT affair as an example of the Nixon administration's readiness to make special deals with big corporate election supporters. "Four years ago," the congressman said emotionally, "an enterprising author wrote *The Selling of the President* about Richard Nixon. Now we are confronted with 'The Selling of the U.S. Government' by Richard Nixon."

In March, 1974, Special Watergate Prosecutor Leon Jaworski included Kroc's campaign gift in his investigation of illegal political influences. But after some debate, House Judiciary Chairman Peter Rodino decided to drop McDonald's from the impeachment investigation. The President's supporters applauded this decision, but it was denounced by Representative Elizabeth Holtzman of New York, who urged that the House Judiciary Committee further consider the hamburger money as additional grounds for removal of the President from office. It never was.

Another controversy involved the minimum wage. On May 11, 1972, the U.S. House of Representatives passed a piece of legislation that some congressional wags and others referred to as the "McDonald's bill." On the House floor, however, it had been an item of bitter debate, and the Senate a few weeks later refused to pass it, deadlocking the issue for the rest of the year. The "McDonald's bill" called for a subminimum wage, that is a "youth differential" which would allow employers to hire sixteen- and seventeen-year-old workers, as well as full-time students, at 80 percent of the newly proposed minimum wage.

President Nixon had backed the "youth differential" because it was anti-inflationary, he said, and because raising the federal minimum wage for teen-agers would drive their unemployment rate higher. In Congress, Nixon's subminimum wage allies were mainly Republicans and Southern Democrats. The bill would be of benefit to McDonald's for the obvious reason that, as the largest employer of working youngsters and students in the country, it would save millions in labor costs.

In the election year of 1972, for the first time, an actual hamburger lobby descended on Capitol Hill. The lobbyists sought out key House members to dissuade them from going along with the Senate's rejection of the "youth differential." Because of the differences between the Senate and House versions on the reduced rate for youth, no minimum-wage bill was passed that year.

The activities of McDonald's in Washington did not escape columnist Jack Anderson. In September, 1972, he reported Ray Kroc's contribution of "a whopping $255,000" to reelect Nixon and linked this to the fact that both the administration and McDonald's had been working simultaneously to keep a "regressive youth rate" in the minimum-wage bill. The Hamburger King "vigorously" denied that his political generosity had anything to do with McDonald's lobbying drive to hold down the pay for its youthful workers. His contribution was not designed to influence the White House, Kroc told one of Anderson's reporters; the money had been given, he said, merely to buy "some insurance in the free enterprise system, in which I strongly believe."

McDonald's open lobbying for the subminimum wage in Congress and the White House complemented its campaign in the hamburger stands in the field. Organized labor was adamantly opposed to the "youth differential" and urged members of Congress to defeat the provision. It argued that the $1.60 minimum wage had been in effect since 1968, and that at the time of the congressional debate it was worth only $1.25 in purchasing power. The AFL–CIO said that inflation was not caused by minimum wages, and it cited the Department of Labor's own statistics to challenge Nixon's claim that raising the minimum wage for youngsters would cause the loss of their jobs.

Consumer, farmer, minority, and student groups joined organized labor in fighting a subminimum wage, which according to the Nixon plan would pay less not only to youth but also to domestics and farm workers, whose legal minimum wage was still $1.30 an hour. In the vanguard of the attack was the National Student Lobby. "The administration . . . is pushing a proposal to pay a lower minimum wage to job seekers aged sixteen to seventeen," the Washington-based student office said in an open message to Congress called "Young Americans Need Your Help." "Why should these young workers be forced to work for less than other workers? Why should an employer be encouraged to fire a father so he can save forty cents an hour by hiring a son or daughter?"

Anti-McDonald's campaigns quietly got under way at a number of campuses. Posters began appearing showing Ronald McDonald holding a sign that said "Boycott McDonald's." Some of the posters were brought onto the floor of the House of Representatives by Democratic Congressman John Dent of Pennsylvania, member of the House Education and Labor subcommittee. Dent characterized the Nixon proposals as showing "a very callous disregard for youth," and he vowed that he would never approve a bill that paid youngsters less than the regular basic rate.

Congressman Dent's legislative assistant, John Vagley, was impressed by the intensity of the petitioners; by their crusading zeal and their efforts to enlist the sympathies of the members of the Rules Committee. But what Vagley saw of McDonald's political operations did not fill him with admiration. "These people," Vagley said in an interview, "were trying to pass off the [youth differential] provision under the guise of training people to work, giving people an opportunity to train and to learn a job before you pay them the full minimum wage.

"Hell, what kind of training is involved in pushing a hamburger across the stand. This was just a typical case of the greedy employer who is just down here trying to get his own little oil-depletion allowance that applies only to him, so his profits can rise."

On the floor of the House, the staunchest defender of the "youth differential" was John Erlenborn of Illinois, the ranking Republican member on Dent's Labor subcommittee, who happened to represent the district that included Hamburger Central. Another congressional supporter, Minnesota Republican Albert Quie, offered a "compromise" specifically aimed at Hamburger Central, suggesting that a limit be placed on the number of employees a company could hire under the subminimum wage law; this would mean, Quie told the *Wall Street Journal*, that "McDonald's wouldn't be able to fund their whole operation with the youth differential."

But in June, 1973, in what *The Wall Street Journal* described as "a major victory for organized labor," the House passed a bill that would raise the federal minimum wage for most workers from $1.60 to $2.00 in 1973 and $2.20 an hour in 1974. The bill rejected a lower minimum wage for sixteen- and seventeen-year-olds, though it still allowed employers to pay less to full-time students doing part-time work, as well as to domestics and farm workers. The House bill was passed by the Senate and, as expected, it was vetoed by Nixon.

The President adamantly insisted on the "youth differential" and proposed a magnanimous increase in the subminimum wages of domestics and farm workers from $1.30 to $1.50 an hour, and suggested generally raising the minimum to $2.00 in 1974.

Congressman John Dent castigated the Nixon proposals,

saying it would put "our youth back into the mines and the mills of this country." George Meany, president of the AFL–CIO, declared, "The will of the majority has again been thwarted and the worst-paid workers in America will continue to subsidize their greedy employers."

Horatio Hamburger

"I Wanna See Some Guy Goin' Crazy!"

Previous winners of the award ranged from former President Herbert Hoover to merchandizing king J. C. Penney, World War I flying ace Eddie Rickenbacker, and comedian Bob Hope. At the Waldorf Astoria in 1972, Dr. Norman Vincent Peale made the presentation to Ray Kroc. The inscription on his Horatio Alger trophy read: "Towards the Enhancing of the American Tradition of Overcoming Obstacles to Achieve Success through Diligence, Industry, Perseverance."

It was one of many. Honors and recognition have come to gladden Ray Kroc's old age. He has received perhaps more Good Scout awards from Boy Scout troops than any other living American. He has been cited for his support of SOAR—Save Our American Resources. He has been named "Marketing Man of the Year," "Mr. Pickle," and honorary citizen of the potato state of Idaho. He has been given the Golden Plate Award from the food-service industry; a personal membership in the Missionary Association of Mary Immaculate; and the

Victoria Denise Deron Award from the Special Olympics for mentally handicapped children. Early in '73 the Lions International named him "American of the Year," presenting the award at half time during the American Bowl football game between the North and South in Tampa, Florida.

On the occasion of his seventieth birthday the founder of McDonald's announced that it was his greatest pleasure to "share his good fortune with others." With much fanfare a press bulletin was released revealing that Ray Kroc had given away $7.5 million in burger stock.

Among the beneficiaries of Kroc's philanthropy were the Great Ape House at Chicago's Lincoln Park Zoo, the Universe Theater at the Adler Planetarium, an exhibit of ecological problems at the Field Museum of Natural History, the Passavant Memorial Hospital for studies in prenatal and postnatal birth defects, and the PACE Institute of Cook County Jail for a rehabilitation program. The more than a dozen other organizations that received gifts included TV star Danny Thomas's special charity, the St. Jude's Children's Research Hospital in Memphis for children suffering from leukemia; the Harvard Church in Oak Park, Illinois, which Ray Kroc attended as a child; and the Public Library in Rapid City, South Dakota, of which his wife was a trustee.

Thus, from the vantage of his three-score years and ten, Ray Kroc could look back on a life where in the end it had all worked out for the best. He was a millionaire hundreds of times over. His homes were staffed with cooks, caretakers, and chauffeurs. He could fly anywhere in the world in his own jet and he had wealth, honors, and recognition. He had been personally invited to the White House to meet President Nixon and it had all worked out so well that even his final and fondest dream came true when in early 1974 he bought the San Diego Padres, a ball club that had lost five hundred games in five years.

Ray Kroc had been a self-described baseball nut since the

age of seven, when his father took him to see his first ball game. He had been a fan of the Chicago Cubs since 1909, had watched the Cubs play their first World Series against the Boston Red Sox, and had seen Babe Ruth and all the baseball greats. When he came into his millions he immediately launched the first of many attempts to buy the Cubs. But the Cubs were owned by P. K. Wrigley, the chewing-gum heir, and P. K. Wrigley liked to watch his team on TV in the six-teenth-floor office of the Wrigley Building in Chicago.

Kroc's purchase of the Padres acquainted many Americans for the first time with the man behind the hamburger, espe-cially as the baseball season proceeded and the Padres sank deeper into their familiar National League cellar spot. Kroc's name was in the news. He was interviewed and sought out when it became apparent that he was a genuine character, a throwback to another time when plutocrats unabashedly re-galed the country with their antics.

Kroc landed in the national news almost from the very be-ginning of the baseball season. The most widely reported inci-dent occurred during the Padres' disastrous home opener against the Houston Astros, when Ray Kroc grabbed the pub-lic-address mike up in his owner's booth at San Diego Stadium and before forty thousand screaming, jumping fans (including one naked streaker) shouted, "I have never seen such stupid ball-playing in my life!"

During the rest of the season he delighted the fans by giving away a free ticket to anyone who showed up wearing a cook's hat and could prove that he was a hamburger cook. During a Padres' home game against the Montreal Expos, Kroc threw $10,000 into the field, inviting people from the stands to scramble for the bills. And the stunts paid off, even though the Padres performed as dismally as before. A record number of fans showed up to watch the games—and hopefully another unpredictable performance by the irrepressible Hamburger King.

In his efforts to spice up the game, Kroc had borrowed a

leaf from his old friend Bill Veeck, a former Chicago Cub fan and ball club owner. Veeck had livened up the game with a carnival atmosphere, bringing excitement to his listless Saint Louis Browns, as well as a marked rise in attendance. He would entertain audiences by sending a midget in to bat, giving away unlabeled cans of vegetables as prizes and by instituting "Grandstand Managers' Day," which had fans responding to signs hoisted from the field asking, "Infield In?" or "Should We Walk Him?"

Ray Kroc, too, complained in the San Diego press that baseball had "lost some of its excitement, some of its allure." He deplored the fact that baseball's patron saint, Leo Durocher, could sit on a corner of the Cubs' bench in Chicago and look the same losing or winning. Kroc wanted to see a coach or owner get in back of the dugout, screaming. At a press conference he criticised P. K. Wrigley for never showing up at spring training or at the Cubs' home games. Kroc said he wanted to inject new life into the game. *"I wanna see some guy goin' crazy!"* he rasped.

When the Hamburger King bought the Padres he brought to his new enterprise all his customary enthusiasm. Kroc's stunts had people talking not just about baseball but about McDonald's. The Padres became an unofficial part of Hamburger Central's powerful propaganda apparatus. This was made clear by Ray Kroc during the San Diego press conference at which he announced his purchase of the local team. The Hamburger King is said to have looked sporty and spry, a small gent wearing a dashing blue blazer, a dark polka-dot shirt, and a snazzy ascot propped under a shiny pink jaw.

Ray Kroc reportedly entered the press conference area leaning on a cane. Sometimes in the morning he needed help to get his right hip up, and the cane buttressed the hip when his arthritis was severe. Kroc was also troubled by diabetes, forcing him to limit the intake of his own hamburgers. The Kroc Foundation headquartered at his California ranch funded research at the University of Saint Louis to study arthritis and diabetes, as well as multiple sclerosis, from which his sister suffers. These are the diseases, Kroc once said mournfully, that "kill you inch by inch."

But his acquisition of the Padres again had him fired up and he apparently beamed with vigor and confidence. The press would describe him the next day as a "pixie who brings laughter into a room."

He announced to the sports writers that he would like to see some changes made in baseball, like starting the game at four or five in the afternoon so as not to foul up the "conventioneers and every restaurant and steak house in town." He had also thought of a "package deal" for a party of people, who would come to the ball park on a bus and get a box seat, cocktails, and dinner, and afterward have the bus take them back. He talked at length about selling beer in the stands, even to minors who were prohibited from buying it by impractical laws. "Holy Kripes!" Kroc snorted, "what the hell is the difference if somebody goes up to the counter and hands it to a minor?"

In 1970 the first McDonald's to sell over one million dollars' worth of hamburgers a year had been the stand in Bloomington, Minnesota. The outlet was located in a sports complex housing the Minnesota Twins, Vikings, and North Stars. McDonald's Bloomington volume had proved that sports fans were insatiable hamburger eaters. The traditional baseball fare of hot dogs and beer was about to be ousted by the new "All-American" baseball meal of hamburgers and beer. The Hamburger King revealed to the press people that he had a few ideas about picking up fans for the Padres and, incidentally, a few customers for McDonald's.

"We have to get some salesmen out. We have to get word-a-mouth. Proud people who are boosters, who sell each other. And I think this is a psychological thing. I think they are there and they want to be interested in a good, clean sport. And all it takes is a little *shuck,* so we're gonna try and do that. When we're playing the Cubs in Chicago, for instance. We got about two hundred McDonald's in Chicago. We'll do something like giving every youngster a free Big Mac and a McDonald's hat.

"So we'll have a hell of a lot of youngsters in the stands with McDonald's hats on, who are gonna. . . ."